YATRA
Rohit Ghai

First published in the UK and USA in 2025 by
Nourish, an imprint of Watkins Media Limited
Unit 11, Shepperton House, 83–93 Shepperton Road, London
N1 3DF

enquiries@nourishbooks.com

Design and typography copyright
© Watkins Media Limited 2025
Text © Rohit Ghai 2025
Photography copyright © Gareth Morgans 2025
Location photography copyright © Shutterstock 2025
Illustration copyright © Shutterstock 2025

The right of Rohit Ghai to be identified as the Author of this text has been asserted in accordance with the Copyright, Designs and Patents Act of 1988.

All rights reserved. No part of this book may be reproduced in any form or by any electronic or mechanical means, including information storage and retrieval systems, without permission in writing from the publisher, except by a reviewer who may quote brief passages in a review.

Publisher: Fiona Robertson
Commissioning Editor: Ella Chappell
Project Editor: Emily Preece-Morrison
Head of Design & Art Direction: Karen Smith
Typesetting: Eleri Stanton
Production: Uzma Taj
Commissioned Photography: Gareth Morgans
Photography Assistant: Becci Hutchings
Food Stylist: Jennifer Joyce
Prop Stylist: Julie Patmore

A CIP record for this book is available from the British Library
ISBN: 978-1-84899-435-5 (Hardback)
ISBN: 978-1-84899-436-2 (eBook)

10 9 8 7 6 5 4 3 2 1

Typeset in Brandon Grotesque
Printed in Bosnia and Herzegovina

Publisher's note
While every care has been taken in compiling the recipes for this book, Watkins Media Limited, or any other persons who have been involved in working on this publication, cannot accept responsibility for any errors or omissions, inadvertent or not, that may be found in the recipes or text, nor for any problems that may arise as a result of preparing one of these recipes. If you are pregnant or breastfeeding or have any special dietary requirements or medical conditions, it is advisable to consult a medical professional before following any of the recipes contained in this book.

Notes on the recipes
Unless otherwise stated:
Use medium fruit and vegetables
Use fresh herbs, spices and chillies
Do not mix metric, imperial and US cup measurements:
1 tsp = 5ml 1 tbsp = 15ml 1 cup = 250ml

nourishbooks.com

YATRA

A culinary journey across India

Michelin-starred
Rohit Ghai

CONTENTS

INTRODUCTION 6
BASIC RECIPES 12

PUNJAB 22
UTTAR PRADESH 44
BIHAR 68
WEST BENGAL 88
ANDHRA PRADESH 110
KERALA 130
GOA 150
MAHARASHTRA 170
GUJARAT 192
RAJASTHAN 212

ABOUT THE AUTHOR 232
ACKNOWLEDGEMENTS 233
INDEX 234

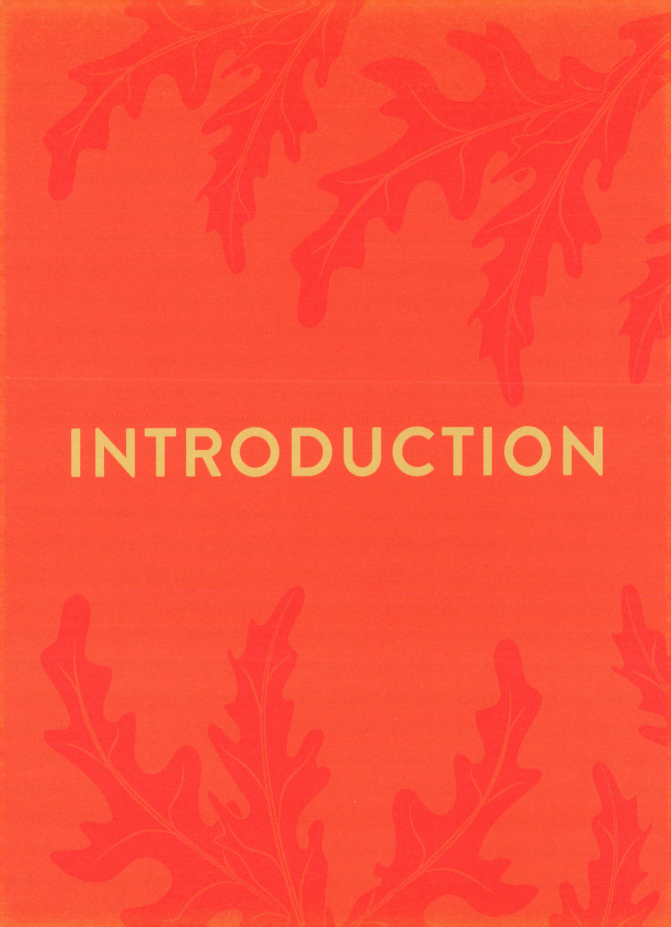

INTRODUCTION

A CULINARY JOURNEY

This book is very personal to me. The word *yatra* means "journey" or "pilgrimage" in Urdu, and I wanted this book to symbolize a journey around my homeland, encompassing the many taste experiences I have had the fortune to enjoy there. India is a vast land with at least 26 different regional cuisines – discovering them is a joy.

This book features diverse and creative dishes, influenced by my favourite places, from arid Rajasthan, punctuated by grand palaces, to the rain-rich soils of Bengal; from green, luscious regions like Kerala, with its abundance of fresh vegetables, to my beloved Punjab, where they cook with heart and soul. Put them together and you have a fiery cuisine, full of life. These varied environments have shaped the culture, cuisines and flavours bursting onto people's plates. It is the wonderful diversity of what can be found from region to region that excites me. I've chosen ten different areas to explore and a handful of recipes from each region offer a window into the culinary delights each extraordinary place has to offer.

Indian food has a lot of depth and complexity in flavour and I think that sometimes leads to the notion that our recipes are over-complicated to make. I have written this book to dispel this idea, as the dishes we cook at home are often very simple. These are tried and tested, authentic home-style recipes, designed to bring families together. I have tried to choose dishes that showcase the depth of flavour Indian food is famous for, that are also easy to make. You will find something to suit all tastes, from meat to seafood or vegetarian recipes. There are starters and sides, a few signature Indian bread preparations and some delicious chutneys and pickles to liven up every meal. I have also included at least one or two traditional Indian desserts, particular to each region, for something different at the dinner table.

I am forever inspired by the wondrous variety in Indian cuisines. Wherever you choose to travel you will find something new to excite your tastebuds. I start the journey in my homeland, the northern region of **Punjab**, where dairy farming predominates and you will discover a wealth of rich, buttery, creamy dishes, as well as yogurt drinks – *lassis* – of every kind. Smoky tandoori dishes and breads are another local favourite.

Move east to **Uttar Pradesh** and you will find a huge variety of dishes due to the temperate climate and widely varied landscape. I am always inspired by the colourful use of vegetables in their many *subzis* and classic *korma* dishes.

Further east in **Bihar**, where the Ganges floods its fertile plains, vegetable dishes are varied and not too spicy. Despite the state being largely vegetarian, hearty meat dishes abound.

West Bengal in the northeast, skirting the Himalayas to the north and the Bay of Bengal to the south, is richly diverse and verdant, with a cuisine less reliant on garlic and onions and more liberal in its use of ginger and poppy seeds, with some beautiful fish dishes to explore.

In the eastern region of **Andra Pradesh**, the markets are full of tangy tamarind pods and fiery red chillies, resulting in a cuisine of spicy, hot and surprising flavours – there are many opulent dishes unique to the region, which are not to be missed.

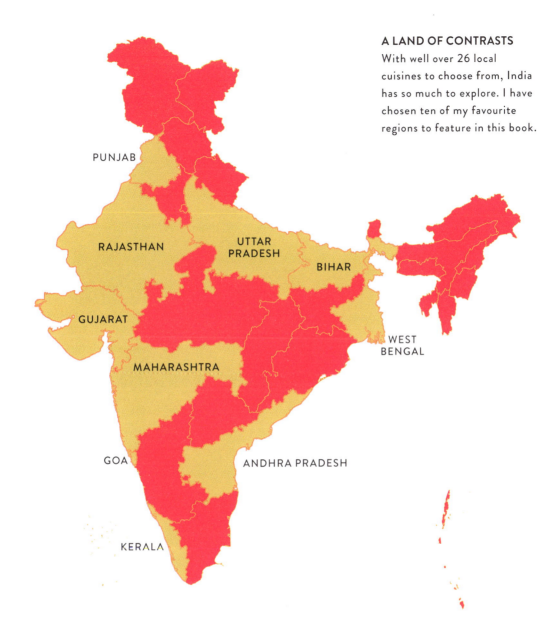

A LAND OF CONTRASTS
With well over 26 local cuisines to choose from, India has so much to explore. I have chosen ten of my favourite regions to feature in this book.

On the southern tip of the peninsula lies **Kerala** – the Malabar coast – where sweet coconuts and delicate spicing rule. Due to its unusually rainy climate, it is lush and green, while its neighbours are more arid, so some beautiful vegetable dishes can be found. Here, you will find some of the few beef dishes prepared in the continent, as well as a fantastic abundance of seafood delights.

The tiny western coast state of **Goa** may be familiar to many from their holidays. Naturally, fish and seafood is the staple offering, but you may be surprised by one of its predominant flavours – vinegar, especially that fermented from the coconut palm. It is here that the world-famous *vindaloo* was born, with its slightly sour and tangy notes.

> For anyone who loves Indian food, this is a must-have cookbook that revels in the diverse treasure trove of Indian cooking.

The vast western region of **Maharashtra**, nicknamed "the gateway of India", is one of India's commercial and agricultural leaders. The metropolitan areas, such as Mumbai, offer many popular street foods and quick bites, while the countryside enjoys rich, heavily spiced curries. Mangoes are the state's fruit and you will find them in so many local dishes.

Gujarat is a region of grandeur, fiercely hot in summer and mild in winter, and popular with tourists, with hill resorts, wildlife sanctuaries, ancient Buddhist caves, temples and a stunning coastline to visit. Vegetarianism is deeply rooted in the culture here, and *dhokla*, the famous savoury steamed sponge cake, is a classic local treat.

Neighbouring **Rajasthan** is arid and dusty, its desert-like landscape dotted with impressive fortified palaces. The scarcity of water led to a uniquely simple and rustic cuisine that is nevertheless creative and delicious. Meat, dried fruits and dairy-based dishes are often eaten with wheat or millet bread, as it is one of the few regions where rice is not a staple.

The sheer breadth of Indian cuisines is astounding when you come to look at them in detail. I find the food of my homeland endlessly exciting – I hope you enjoy exploring it with me.

THE FLAVOURS OF HOME

My first cooking experiences were learnt first-hand from my mother. Her kitchen was the heart of our home, where she would cook for our large family every day. I was the youngest and spent a lot of time with her, observing her cooking and learning her techniques. It was a very basic set-up at home. My mother would say, "Rohit, whatever you cook, if you cook with your heart and soul then you don't need any special ingredients." Her dips and pickles were amazing, as was her *paratha*, cooked on the griddle, which she would serve just with homemade butter. That's all you really need with *paratha*, along with a cup of *chai*.

The ideas I found there in my mother's kitchen have followed me my whole life. Growing up in Punjab, at first my cooking was heavily influenced by the food from the north, as it's the place I did most of my research and recipe development before embarking on my chef's career in the Oberoi hotel group. My dear mother's recipes followed me to the kitchens I have worked in all over the world, and now I bring them to you. Many are condensed in this book so people can create them at home.

Yatra represents the culinary journey of my life and the creative dishes at the heart of my very being. I hope you delight in preparing and eating them, and sharing them with others, as much as I do.

BASIC RECIPES

Masalas/Spice Mixes
Garam Masala
Bengali Garam Masala
Ghati Masala
Kala/Goda Masala
Panch Phoran
Chaat Masala
Poha Magic Masala
Biryani Masala
Kolhapuri Masala

Pastes
Ginger-Garlic Paste
Fried Onion Paste

Chutneys, Pickles and Raita
Mint and Coriander Chutney
Tomato Chutney
Coconut Chutney
Cauliflower Pickle
Burani Raita

Everyday Breads
Naan
Chapati

GARAM MASALA

The garam masala spice blend is the backbone of Indian cuisine – an important mix that is used for nearly all savoury preparations. A combination of 16 whole spices, it is warm and fragrant, and just a pinch will take your dish to the next level. This is my mother's special blend.

Makes 225g/8oz

4–5 whole dried Kashmiri red chillies
5 star anise
½ nutmeg
2 cinnamon sticks
5 black cardamom pods
1½ tbsp green cardamom pods
2½ tbsp cumin seeds
1½ tbsp black cumin seeds
1½ tbsp coriander seeds
1½ tbsp cloves
1½ tbsp black peppercorns
1½ tbsp black stone flower
1 tbsp fennel seeds
1½ tsp fenugreek seeds
2–3 mace blades
4 bay leaves

Heat a heavy, dry frying pan over a low-medium heat and slowly roast each spice individually until it releases its aroma and is hot to touch. Transfer to a large plate and leave to cool.

When cool, grind the roasted spices (in batches) to a fine powder in a spice grinder. Sift the ground spices to remove any large, coarse pieces, and grind those again. Mix the resulting powder together well.

Store in an airtight glass jar for up to 6–8 weeks.

BENGALI GARAM MASALA

Each region of India has their own particular blend of garam masala, which is used for curries and vegetable dishes. Bengali garam masala is a combination of aromatic and delicate whole spices, making a spice mix that is not strong but is very flavourful.

Makes about 50g/1¾oz

2 x 5cm/2in cinnamon sticks
4 tbsp green cardamom pods
2 tbsp cloves
2 tbsp black cumin seeds
1 tsp black peppercorns

Dry-roast the whole spices in a hot frying pan over a medium heat for 3–4 minutes. Remove from the heat and allow to cool completely.

In a spice grinder, grind the cooled whole spices to a fine powder.

Store in an airtight glass jar. The mix will keep fresh and fragrant for up to 4–6 weeks.

GHATI MASALA

Ghati masala is one of my favourite spice mixes – it goes very well with my signature dish of crispy fried prawns (see Ghati Masala Prawns, page 180) and is essential for dishes like *Vada Pav* (see page 176). This is a Maharashtrian mix (named for the *ghats* – mountain passes – of the region). It is worth making your own fresh spice mix rather than buying it from the market, as the flavour will be so much better.

Makes about 150g/5oz

1 tsp rapeseed/canola oil
8 garlic cloves, peeled
50g/1¾oz grated dried coconut
1 tbsp sesame seeds
1 tbsp roasted unsalted peanuts
2 tsp Kashmiri chilli powder
1 tsp ground coriander
½ tsp tamarind paste
salt, to taste

Heat the oil in a frying pan over a low heat and roast the garlic cloves for 1 minute. Remove the garlic with a slotted spoon to a plate and wipe out the pan with kitchen paper.

In the same pan, dry-roast the coconut and sesame seeds over a low heat until the sesame seeds start to pop (about 30 seconds), then transfer to the same plate as the garlic and leave to cool for 5 minutes.

Add the cooled garlic, coconut and sesame seeds to a spice grinder or food processor along with the other ingredients and grind to a medium coarse consistency. It will be slighter wetter than a powder but not quite a paste. Taste for salt and add more if required.

Store in an airtight container for up to 4–6 weeks in the refrigerator.

BASIC RECIPES

KALA MASALA

This is another very famous Maharashtrian spice mix, which goes by two names: kala or goda masala. *Goda* means "sweet" and *kala* means "black" in Marathi. The two mixes are very similar, but the sweet element in goda comes from the use of coconut, which I omit here. The flavourful kala masala spice mix is indeed a very dark brown, almost black, colour, as the whole spices are roasted until they are very dark before grinding.

Makes about 225g/8oz

4 tbsp rapeseed/canola oil, for frying
15g/½oz whole dried red chillies
15 bay leaves
3 whole nutmegs (12g/½oz)
12g/½oz star anise
10g/⅓oz cinnamon sticks
25g/1oz coriander seeds
25g/1oz black cumin seeds
25g/1oz cumin seeds
25g/1oz black peppercorns
12g/½oz Szechuan peppercorns
25g/1oz black cardamom pods
12g/½oz green cardamom pods
20g/¾oz cloves
6g/¼oz black stone flower
6g/¼oz mace

Heat the oil in a sauté pan, add all the whole spices and shallow-fry over a medium heat, stirring frequently, until aromatic. When the spices are darkly browned or blackened (but before they burn), remove from the heat and strain through a sieve (discarding the oil). Leave to cool.

Transfer all the cooled spices to a spice grinder or food processor and grind to a coarse, slightly wet powder (any large pieces that refuse to grind can be ground again, or discarded).

Store in an airtight jar for up to 6–8 weeks.

PANCH PHORAN

A classic Bengali mix of five whole seed spices. The seeds are never ground in this blend. It's great for pickling vegetables (see Cauliflower Pickle on page 20) or for adding flavour to dals (see *Masoor Dal* on page 104), curries, soups or salads.

Makes about 40g/1½oz

2 tsp fennel seeds
3 tsp cumin seeds
1 tsp onion seeds
2 tsp mustard seeds
1 tsp fenugreek seeds

Simply mix all the ingredients together and store in an airtight container for up to 3 months.

CHAAT MASALA

This tangy powdered spice mix is a combination of dried mango, cumin, coriander, dried ginger, dried mint, asafoetida, black salt, table salt and black peppercorns. It is typically used as a seasoning for salads and kebabs.

Makes about 200g/7oz

25g/1oz cumin seeds
25g/1oz black peppercorns
20g/¾oz black salt
20g/¾oz dried pomegranate seeds
15g/½oz dried mint
2 tsp carom seeds/ajwain
2 tsp fenugreek seeds
75g/3oz dried mango powder/amchur
15g/½oz ground ginger
15g/½oz salt
1½ tsp Kashmiri chilli powder
½ tsp asafoetida

Put the cumin seeds, peppercorns, black salt, dried pomegranate seeds, dried mint, carom seeds and fenugreek seeds in a spice grinder and grind to a fine powder. Transfer to a bowl, add the remaining ingredients and mix well. Sift to remove any large pieces.

Store in an airtight container for up to 6–8 weeks.

POHA MAGIC MASALA

I came across this spice mix during a visit to Indore, one of the foodie cities in Madhya Pradesh, where I first tried the masala in a dish of *Poha* (see page 175). It has a pungent, savoury taste, which intensifies the flavour of poha (flattened rice). I have used this spice mix for *bhel puri* and kebabs, too.

Makes about 50g/1¾oz

1½ tsp cumin seeds
1½ tsp fennel seeds
1 tsp coriander seeds
1 black cardamom pod
3 cloves
a small piece of nutmeg
½ mace blade
1 bay leaf
1½ tsp dried mango powder/amchur
1 tsp Kashmiri chilli powder
½ tsp ground ginger
½ tsp black salt
¼ tsp ground cinnamon
pinch of asafoetida

In a hot, dry frying pan, dry-roast the cumin, fennel and coriander seeds, black cardamom pod, cloves, nutmeg, mace and bay leaf over a medium heat until they begin to smell aromatic. Remove from the heat and spread over a plate to cool.

Transfer the cooled spices to a spice grinder along with the remaining powdered spices and grind to a fine powder.

Store in an airtight container for up to 4–6 weeks.

BIRYANI MASALA

This combination of aromatic whole spices is the ideal blend for biryanis, but it can also be used for kebabs and curries.

Makes about 50g/1¾oz

2–3 bay leaves
2–3 star anise
15 green cardamom pods
2–3 black cardamom pods
2 tbsp black cumin seeds
1½ tbsp fennel seeds
1 tsp black peppercorns
1 mace blade
½ nutmeg
2–3 pieces of black stone flower

In a hot, dry frying pan, dry-roast all the spices over a medium heat until they begin to smell aromatic, about 5–6 minutes. Remove from the heat and spread over a plate to cool.

Transfer the cooled spices to a spice grinder and grind to a fine powder.

Store in an airtight container for up to 4–6 weeks.

KOLHAPURI MASALA

This spicy, earthy masala that hails from the city of Kolhapur will add an authentic touch when cooking Maharashtrian cuisine. You can use it in many curry or vegetable dishes. If you think it's too spicy for you, you can balance it out with some tomato purée/paste or tamarind water.

Makes about 100g/3½oz

2 tbsp rapeseed/canola oil
1 onion, roughly chopped
10 garlic cloves, peeled
100g/3½oz fresh coriander/
  cilantro leaves
50g/1¾oz hot red chilli powder
salt, to taste

SPICE MIX
150g/5oz coriander seeds
1 tbsp cumin seeds
100g/3½oz desiccated coconut
1 tbsp sesame seeds
2 tbsp black peppercorns
1cm (½in) piece of cinnamon
  stick
2 tbsp poppy seeds
1 tsp fenugreek seeds
1 tsp fennel seeds

In a dry, heavy pan, roast the spice mix ingredients over a low heat until aromatic. Transfer to a bowl to cool.

Add the oil to the same pan and heat over a medium heat. Add the onion and garlic and sauté until lightly browned. Remove from the heat and leave to cool slightly.

Transfer all of the ingredients, including the coriander and chilli powder, to a food processor and blitz to a smooth paste. Check the salt and adjust accordingly.

Store in an airtight container in the refrigerator for up to 1 week.

GINGER-GARLIC PASTE

This simple paste of fresh ginger and garlic plays a very important role in Indian cuisine. It is used in everything from curries to marinades for seafood, meat and vegetables. Blending a large batch in advance to store in the refrigerator for whenever you need it is a great time-saver.

Makes 400g/14oz

250g/9oz fresh root ginger
250g/9oz garlic cloves
1 tsp salt
3 tbsp rapeseed/canola oil

Rinse the ginger root under cold running water, then peel and roughly chop. Peel the garlic.

Place the chopped ginger and peeled garlic into a bowl and pour over enough water to cover. Leave to soak for at least 1 hour, then drain.

Transfer the soaked ginger and garlic to a blender, add the salt and oil and blend to a smooth paste.

Transfer the paste to a clean glass jar or other airtight container, seal with the lid and refrigerate. It will keep for up to 4–6 weeks.

FRIED ONION PASTE

This aromatic paste of slowly fried onions mixed with creamy yogurt makes a lovely smooth base to add to curries. It will impart a lovely caramelized flavour to your dishes. I use it in Rajasthani *Kesar Murgh* (see page 228) for added richness.

Makes about 400g/14oz

350ml/12fl oz/scant 1½ cups rapeseed/canola oil
1kg/2lb 4oz onions, finely sliced
100g/3½oz/⅓ cup plain yogurt
1 tsp salt

Heat the oil in a large, heavy pan over a medium heat. Add the sliced onions and slowly sauté, stirring frequently, until well browned and caramelized. Use a slotted spoon to transfer the onions to a tray and spread out to cool down.

When cool, transfer the onions to a blender, add the yogurt and salt, and blitz to a fine paste.

Store in an airtight container in the refrigerator for up to 2 weeks.

MINT AND CORIANDER CHUTNEY

My mother use to make this refreshing chutney, also known as *hari* (green) chutney, in a pestle and mortar at home. Today, we make it in a blender to get a lovely smooth texture. It's as popular in India as it is elsewhere – most Indian restaurants nowadays will serve a mint chutney with poppadums, kebabs and snacks.

Serves 6–8

30g/1oz fresh mint, leaves only
50g/1¾oz fresh coriander/cilantro, leaves and stems
2 tbsp roughly chopped fresh root ginger
3–4 garlic cloves, peeled
2 green chillies
¼ tsp roasted ground cumin
1 tbsp granulated sugar
½ tsp salt
2 tbsp rapeseed/canola oil
½ tsp Chaat Masala (store-bought or see page 15)
2 tbsp lime juice

Thoroughly wash the mint and coriander in a large bowl of water, then drain.

Transfer to a blender and add the ginger, garlic, green chillies, roasted ground cumin, sugar, salt and oil. Blend to a fine paste.

Add the chaat masala and lime juice, and mix well before serving. It will keep, covered, in the refrigerator for up to 4–5 days.

COCONUT CHUTNEY

Coconut chutney is a popular dip in southern India that is served with most snacks and *dosa*. This is a very simple way to make it at home.

Serves 6–8

2 tbsp rapeseed/canola oil
8–10 curry leaves
4–5 green chillies, slit
30g/1oz chana dal (or roasted chana dal)
20g/¾oz fresh root ginger, peeled and grated
200g/7oz fresh coconut (skinless), grated
salt, to taste

TEMPERING

1 tbsp rapeseed/canola oil
2 dried red chillies
1 tsp mustard seeds
8–10 curry leaves
pinch of asafoetida

Heat the oil in a saucepan over a medium heat. Add the curry leaves, green chillies, chana dal, ginger and grated coconut, and sauté for 8–10 minutes. Remove from the heat and transfer to a bowl to cool.

Transfer the cooled mixture to a blender and blitz to a fine paste, adding a little water if required. Transfer to a bowl.

For the tempering, heat the oil in a small pan over a medium heat and add the chillies, mustard seeds and curry leaves. Once they start crackling, add the asafoetida and mix well. Pour the tempering over the coconut chutney and mix well. Adjust the salt to taste and serve with snacks.

Store in an airtight container in the refrigerator for up to 1 week.

TOMATO CHUTNEY

This is a great chutney to serve with snacks. It's quick and easy to make and can be served without the tempering if you want something in a hurry – although it's extra delicious with it.

Serves 6–8

1 tbsp rapeseed/canola oil
1 tbsp chana dal/Bengal gram
4–6 dried Kashmiri chillies
2 fresh green chillies, slit
⅛ tsp ground turmeric
3 medium–large tomatoes, roughly chopped
2 tbsp chopped fresh coriander/cilantro stems
2 tbsp roughly chopped fresh root ginger
4–5 garlic cloves, peeled
1 sprig of curry leaves
salt, to taste

TEMPERING (OPTIONAL)

1 tsp rapeseed/canola oil
½ tsp mustard seeds
1 tsp urad dal
1 sprig of curry leaves
1 dried red chilli, broken in half
pinch of asafoetida

Heat the oil in a medium saucepan over a medium heat. Add the chana dal and sauté until aromatic and deeply golden. Add the dried red chillies, fresh green chillies and turmeric along with a pinch of salt, and sauté for a further 1–2 minutes. Add the tomatoes, coriander stems, ginger and garlic cloves along with the sprig of curry leaves, and sauté until the tomatoes are soft and mushy. Remove from the heat and leave to cool.

Transfer the cooled mixture to a food processor and blend until smooth (you may need to add a little water if it is too thick). Taste the chutney and add more salt, if needed.

To temper the chutney, heat the oil in a medium pan over a medium heat. Add the mustard seeds and urad dal, and sauté until the dal turns golden. Add the curry leaves and dried chilli and sauté until the curry leaves turn crisp. Stir in the asafoetida, then either stir the chutney directly into the pan or pour this tempering over the tomato chutney in a bowl.

Mix well and serve.

CAULIFLOWER PICKLE

This is an easy, home-style recipe for a lovely sweet and sour pickle. You can use this same pickling liquor to pickle most vegetables. If you prefer a spicy, garlicky flavour to your pickle, you can cut down the sweetness by reducing the sugar and jaggery and add more of the chilli powder and garlic when making the liquor.

Makes about 450g/1lb

1 cauliflower, cut into small florets
100ml/3½fl oz/scant ½ cup mustard oil
1 tbsp Panch Phoran (store-bought or see page 14)
60g/2oz/5 tbsp granulated sugar
40g/1½oz/3 heaped tbsp jaggery (or palm sugar)
100ml/3½fl oz/scant ½ cup white wine vinegar
1 tbsp ground coriander
1 tsp ground turmeric
1 tsp hot red chilli powder
½ tsp asafoetida
1½ tsp salt, or to taste

Blanch the cauliflower florets in salted boiling water for 3–4 minutes, then drain and set aside.

Heat the mustard oil in a medium pan until smoking, then reduce the heat to medium and add the panch phoran. Once crackling, add the remaining ingredients and mix well. Cook until it has reduced by half, about 10–15 minutes.

Pack the cauliflower florets into a large clean jar, pour over the hot pickling liquor and seal with the lid. Set aside for 3–4 days to mature. Store in the refrigerator for 3–4 weeks.

BURANI RAITA

This raita is traditionally served with the biryanis of Hyderabadi cuisine (see page 120), but it is also good with pulao or any Indian meal. Flavoured with garlic and roasted ground cumin, it is an easy and quick raita to make. If you like, you can add chopped onion and cucumber too, to add to the flavour.

Serves 5

250g/9oz/1 cup plain yogurt
½ tsp Ginger-Garlic Paste (see page 17)
1 tbsp rapeseed/canola oil
2–4 garlic cloves, crushed
1 tbsp chopped fresh coriander/cilantro
1 tsp chopped fresh green chilli
¼ tsp roasted ground cumin
salt, to taste

In a mixing bowl, combine the yogurt with the ginger-garlic paste and whisk until smooth.

Heat the oil in a small pan over a medium heat, add the chopped garlic and sauté until golden. Remove from the pan and let cool.

Add the fried garlic along with the remaining ingredients to the yogurt mixture and mix well. Taste for seasoning. (If adding any extra ingredients, add them at this point.)

You can serve the raita immediately or chill it in the refrigerator before serving.

NAAN

A simple, delicious bread made with refined wheat flour, this is traditionally cooked in a charcoal or gas tandoor oven, but I have given you a regular oven method here for ease.

Makes 6–8 breads

500g/1lb 2oz/4 cups refined white/self-raising flour, plus extra for dusting
pinch of salt
1 tsp baking powder
1 egg
2 heaped tsp granulated sugar
100ml/3½fl oz/scant ½ cup milk
150ml/5fl oz/⅔ cup water
rapeseed/canola oil, for greasing

Sift the flour with the salt and baking powder in a large bowl.

Break the egg into a separate small bowl, add the sugar and milk, and mix well.

Make a well in the flour mixture and slowly add the water mixing to incorporate, then add the egg mixture and mix well. Knead until you have a soft and smooth dough that does not stick to your fingers. Cover with a damp cloth and set aside for 20–30 minutes.

Meanwhile, preheat the oven to 200°C/180°C fan/400°F/Gas 6.

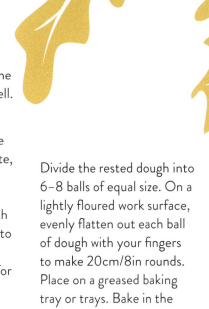

Divide the rested dough into 6–8 balls of equal size. On a lightly floured work surface, evenly flatten out each ball of dough with your fingers to make 20cm/8in rounds. Place on a greased baking tray or trays. Bake in the oven for 7–8 minutes until crisp and lightly browned. Serve hot.

CHAPATI

These simple flatbreads are usually made with wholemeal/wholewheat flour, but my mother used to use a multigrain flour for extra nutrition and would add carom seeds too. Carom seeds help reduce high cholesterol and aid digestion, but they are entirely optional here.

Makes 5–6 chapati

250g/9oz/2 cups wholemeal/wholewheat or multigrain flour
pinch of salt
½ tsp carom seeds/ajwain (optional)
1 tbsp rapeseed/canola oil
up to 150ml/5fl oz/⅔ cup warm water

Sift the flour with the salt in a large bowl. Add the carom seeds, if using, and oil, and mix well. Slowly add half of the warm water and mix with your hands, gradually adding more water just until you have a soft dough. The dough shouldn't be too dry or too wet, so adjust accordingly.

Divide the dough into 5–6 balls of equal size. Use a rolling pin to roll each ball out to a thickness of 2–3mm/⅛in.

Heat a non-stick frying pan or tawa (griddle) over a medium heat until hot, then slide the rolled chapati onto the hot surface and cook for 1–2 minutes until the bread starts to puff up and is lightly patched with brown. Flip over and cook on the other side for 1 minute. Serve with curries or vegetable dishes.

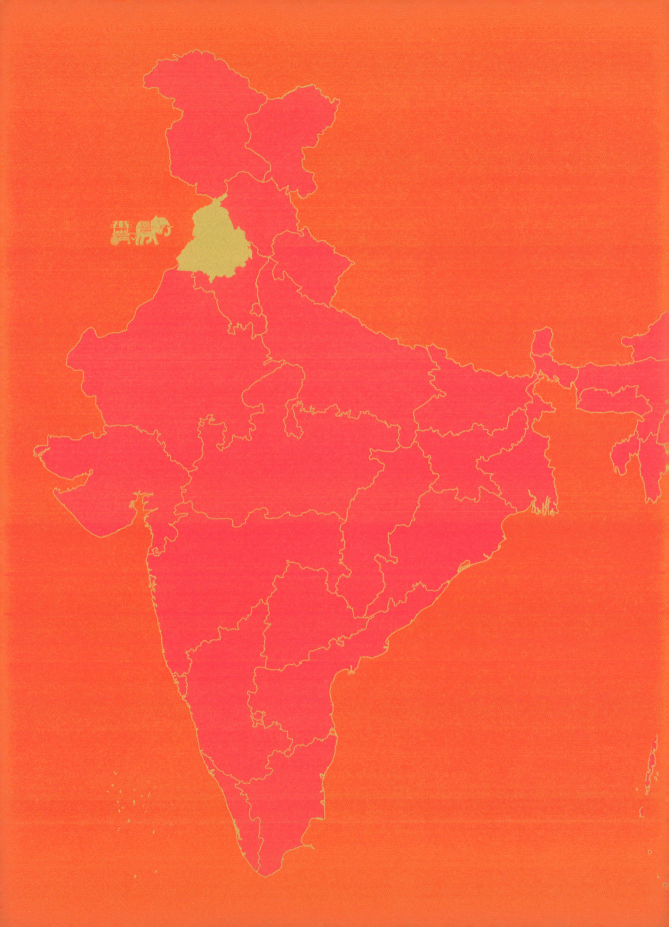

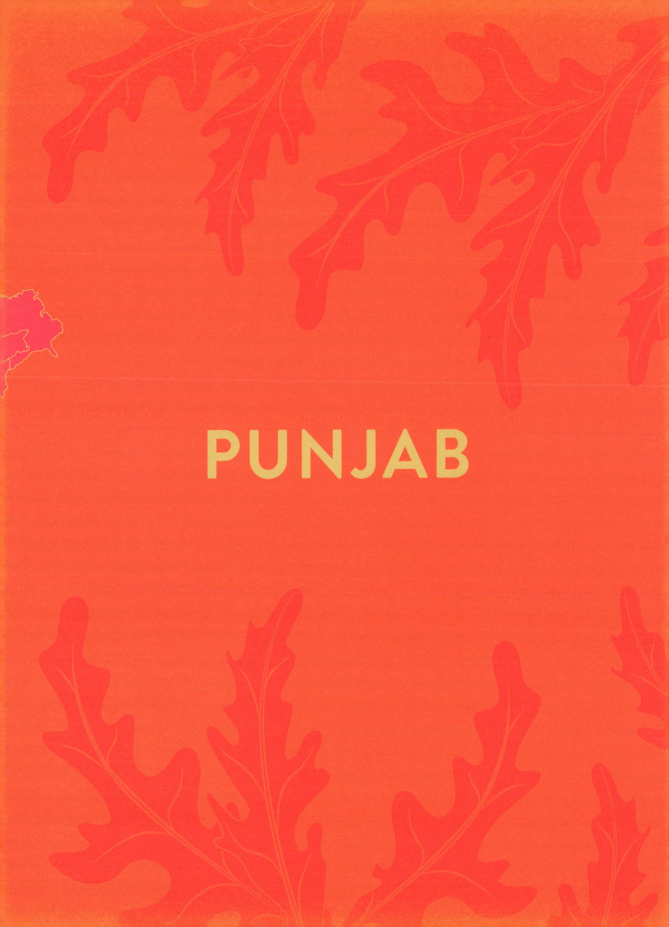

PUNJAB

Punjabis are very passionate about food, and their regional dishes are popular around the world due to their incredible flavours and hearty ingredients. This area in northern India is particularly known for its dairy farming – ghee, cream, milk and yogurt are therefore key ingredients – so rich, buttery sauces and cooling, yogurt-based drinks are a common theme on Punjabi menus.

In the villages, many people still use traditional cooking methods and equipment. Punjabis are most famous throughout India for their tandoori-style cooking, which is named after the *tandoor*: a large, urn-shaped, wood-fired oven, usually made of clay. This produces the soft flatbreads and smoky kebabs that are so loved the world over. Tandoori Chicken is probably one of the most famous of these dishes and can be found on page 28.

I have included some of my favourite Punjabi dishes here: you will find creamy curries, such as Butter Chicken (see page 33) and *Dal Makhani* (page 34); the classic lamb and spinach dish *Saag Gosht* (page 29); and vegetarians will love the *Palak Paneer* (page 39) and kidney-bean dish *Rajma Rasila* (page 30). For dessert, try the delicious *Moong dal Halwa* (page 43). And, of course, no Punjabi meal would be complete without a glass of the famous yogurt drink, Mango *Lassi* (page 40).

AMRITSARI FISH

When I talk about Punjab, I can't help but mention Amritsari fish, which is a very common dish for every Punjabi family. One of my favourite fish dishes, it hails from the city of Amritsar and is so popular that it can be found in any of the local street-food stalls or even the best of hotels. These lightly battered fish pakoras are crunchy, quick to make and light to eat. They are also gluten free. The yogurt is optional as many people in India don't like to have dairy with fish, but it does bring natural sourness and a better flavour to the dish. The rice flour is optional too, but I add it as I think it brings a bit more crunch to the texture.

Serves 4

4 skinless seabass fillets or 600g/1lb 5oz skinless cod fillet, cut into bite-size pieces
300ml/10½fl oz/1¼ cups rapeseed/canola oil, for deep-frying

BATTER

50g/1¾oz/scant ¼ cup plain yogurt (optional)
2 tbsp rice flour (optional)
5 tbsp gram flour/besan
2 tsp Ginger-Garlic Paste (see page 17)
1 tsp carom seeds/ajwain
1 tsp red chilli powder
1–2 tsp salt, to taste
5 tbsp sparkling water, soda water or lager
2 tbsp chopped fresh coriander/cilantro stems
1 tbsp chopped green chillies
1 tbsp chopped fresh root ginger

TO GARNISH

2 fresh limes, halved, for squeezing
1 tsp Chaat Masala (store-bought or see page 15)
1 tbsp chopped fresh coriander/cilantro leaves

In a large bowl, make the batter. Combine the yogurt, flour/s, ginger-garlic paste, spices, salt and water/lager, and mix well to form a lump-free batter. Add the chopped coriander stems, green chillies and ginger, and mix well.

Add the fish pieces to the batter and turn to evenly coat on all sides. Cover the bowl with cling film/plastic wrap or a plate and place in the refrigerator for 15 minutes to marinate.

Heat the oil in a deep, heavy pan or wok over a high heat for about 1 minute, or to 180°C/350°F.

Remove the fish from the refrigerator and carefully lower 2–3 fish pieces at a time into the hot oil. Reduce the heat to medium and fry the fish pieces for about 2 minutes, turning halfway, until crisp and golden brown. Remove with a slotted spoon to a serving bowl and repeat until all the fish pieces are cooked.

Squeeze over some fresh lime juice and sprinkle with chaat masala and chopped coriander leaves. Serve hot.

TANDOORI CHICKEN

Tandoori chicken is a North Indian dish of on-the-bone chicken marinated in yogurt and spices, then charred in a *tandoor*, a cylindrical clay oven. Out of all the kebabs and tandoori preparations, it's fair to say that this dish is "king", which is demonstrated by its popularity across the world.

Serves 4

1 whole chicken (1.2–1.4kg/ 2¾–3¼lb)
50g/1¾oz butter, melted, for greasing and basting

FIRST MARINADE

1 tbsp Ginger-Garlic Paste (see page 17)
1 tbsp lime juice
¼ tsp salt

SECOND MARINADE

200g/7oz/scant 1 cup plain Greek yogurt
2 tbsp mustard oil
1 tsp lime juice
1 tsp Ginger-Garlic Paste (see page 17)
2 tsp Kashmiri chilli powder, or to taste
1 tsp Garam Masala (store-bought or see page 12)
1 tsp ground coriander
1 tsp dried fenugreek leaves
¼ tsp ground turmeric
¼ tsp black salt
1 tbsp chopped fresh coriander/ cilantro stems
½ tsp salt, or to taste

TO SERVE

Mint and Coriander Chutney (see page 18)
onion wedges
lemon wedges

Cut the chicken into 4 pieces, keeping it on the bone. The easiest way to do this is to remove the wing tips with kitchen shears, cut through the skin connecting breast to thigh, then remove the legs; flip the chicken over and remove the backbone with shears, then split the breast in half by cutting through the centre. Make deep gashes over the surface of the chicken pieces and place in a large bowl. Add the ginger-garlic paste, lime juice and salt, and massage well into the gashes in the chicken pieces. Set aside.

In a mixing bowl, combine the ingredients for the second marinade and mix everything well. The marinade has to be thick and not a dripping consistency. Taste and add more salt and chilli powder, if needed.

Add the second marination to the chicken pieces, turning to coat, then cover and refrigerate for at least 6 hours, or overnight if possible.

Bring the chicken back to room temperature before cooking.

Preheat the grill/broiler to its highest setting for at least 15–20 minutes. (Alternatively, cook on skewers over a charcoal barbecue for a smoky flavour.)

Place a greased wire rack in a deep oven tray, then place the marinated chicken pieces on the rack. Grill/broil the chicken for about 15 minutes. Baste the chicken pieces with melted butter on both sides, then grill for another 6–10 minutes, or until the chicken is cooked through. You will need to adjust the timings as it depends on the size of the chicken pieces. Make sure they are nicely charred.

Serve with mint and coriander chutney, and wedges of onion and lemon.

SAAG GOSHT

Another famous delicacy from Punjabi cuisine, soft and succulent pieces of lamb are coated in a mildly spiced spinach gravy. It is such a hearty and comforting dish that North Indians prefer to eat it during winter, usually with *makke ki roti* (maize-flour flatbreads), but you can serve it with any flatbreads. For an alternative option, you can replace the lamb with chicken and follow the same method.

Serves 4

500g/1lb 2oz spinach, washed and drained
100g/3½oz/scant ½ cup ghee or cooking oil
1 tsp cumin seeds
2 bay leaves
2–3 black cardamom pods
2–3 cloves
250g/9oz onions, finely chopped
2 tbsp grated fresh root ginger
5–6 garlic cloves, grated or finely chopped
1–2 green chillies, finely chopped
800g/1lb 12oz boneless lamb, cut into bite-size pieces
1 tsp Kashmiri chilli powder
125g/4½oz tomatoes, finely chopped
1 tsp Garam Masala (store-bought or see page 12)
1 tbsp dried fenugreek leaves
salt, to taste

Bring a large pan of water to the boil, add 1½ teaspoons of salt, then add the spinach and cook for 2–3 minutes. Drain and refresh the spinach in ice-cold water to stop it cooking any further.

Transfer half of the spinach to a blender and blitz to a smooth purée (you may need to add a splash of water to achieve this). Finely chop the remaining spinach. Set both aside.

Heat the ghee or oil in a large pan (that has a lid) over a medium heat. Add the cumin seeds, bay leaves, cardamom pods and cloves, and let them splutter briefly, then add the onions and fry until lightly golden. Add the ginger, garlic and green chillies, and sauté for 1–2 minutes, then add the lamb pieces and mix well. Cook over a high heat until the lamb is browned on all sides.

Add the chilli powder, 1 teaspoon salt and tomatoes and cook for a few minutes until the tomatoes are soft and pulpy. Add the garam masala and fenugreek leaves along with a little water and bring to the boil. Cover and simmer until the lamb is almost cooked, about 20–30 minutes.

Remove the lid, add the chopped spinach and purée and mix well. Check the seasoning. Simmer uncovered for a final 5–6 minutes, or until the curry comes together and reaches the desired consistency.

Serve hot with naan or paratha.

RAJMA RASILA

This is one of my favourite recipes made with kidney beans. My mother used to make it specially on Sundays to celebrate the weekend. It is most delicious and flavourful. In India, legumes are eaten regularly, as they are the main source of protein and fibre. *Dal Tadka*, *Chana Masala*, *Dal Makhani* and *Rajma Masala* are some of the most popular legume preparations from North India, and are always included on Indian restaurant menus or made in most households regularly. I prefer to serve this dish with plain boiled rice alongside *lachha* (sliced onion) and lime wedges.

Serves 4

3 tbsp rapeseed/canola oil
½ tsp cumin seeds
1 small bay leaf
250g/9oz onions, chopped
1½ tsp Ginger-Garlic Paste (see page 17)
50g/1¾oz/scant ¼ cup plain yogurt mixed with 3 tbsp water
1 tsp hot chilli powder
1 tsp Garam Masala (store-bought or see page 12)
1 tsp ground coriander
½ tsp Kashmiri chilli powder
½ tsp dried mango powder/amchur
¼ tsp ground turmeric
100g/3½oz tomato purée/tomato concentrate
2 x 400g/14oz cans of kidney beans, drained and rinsed
400ml/14fl oz/1⅔ cups water, plus extra if needed
1 tsp julienned fresh root ginger
2 fresh tomatoes, diced
2 green chillies, slit
1 tsp dried fenugreek leaves, crushed
salt, to taste
2 tbsp chopped fresh coriander/cilantro leaves, to garnish
sliced red onion and lime wedges, to serve

Heat the oil in a large pan (that has a lid) over a medium heat, and sauté the cumin seeds and bay leaf until they sizzle. Add the chopped onions and cook until just starting to turn golden brown, then add the ginger-garlic paste and cook until the raw smell goes away.

In a small bowl, mix the watered-down yogurt with the ground spices and a good pinch of salt to make a paste. Add this mixture to the pan and sauté until the oil begins to separate. Stir in the tomato purée and cook until the raw smell vanishes. Add the kidney beans, pour in the measured water and stir. Add the ginger, diced tomatoes and slit green chillies, then cover and simmer over a low heat for 10–15 minutes, adding extra water if the mixture gets too dry.

After this time, check whether the kidney beans are completely cooked by mashing a bean – it must be soft. When done, stir in the crushed fenugreek leaves. Taste for seasoning.

Serve garnished with the chopped coriander, with sliced onion and lime wedges on the side, either with plain rice or chapatis.

BUTTER CHICKEN

The famous butter chicken, known as *murgh makhani*, originated in the Punjab. It is a velvety, creamy and flavourful curry made from fresh tomatoes and dairy served with charred, boneless chicken tikka. Its sauce is known for its rich texture and flavours of fenugreek and garlic. This lip-smacking dish is hugely popular the world over.

Serves 4

CHICKEN TIKKA
8–10 boneless, skinless chicken thighs
1 tbsp ginger paste
1 tbsp garlic paste
1 tbsp fresh lime juice
150g/5oz/scant ⅔ cup plain yogurt
4 tbsp Kashmiri red chilli powder
½ tsp garam masala
1 tsp dried fenugreek leaves
1 tbsp mustard oil
salt, to taste

MAKHANI SAUCE
150ml/5fl oz/⅔ cup rapeseed/canola oil
1kg/2¼lb fresh tomatoes, roughly chopped
400g/14oz canned chopped tomatoes
50g/1¾oz fresh root ginger, roughly chopped
50g/1¾oz garlic cloves, crushed
6–8 fresh green chillies, roughly chopped
6–8 green cardamom pods
1 blade mace
1 tbsp cumin seeds
2 bay leaves
1 tbsp Kashmiri chilli powder
50g/1¾oz/2 tbsp honey
100ml/3½fl oz/scant ½ cup double/heavy cream
150g/5oz butter, plus extra to serve
2 tbsp dried fenugreek leaves
salt, to taste

First, coat the chicken thighs with the ginger and garlic pastes, lime juice and a good pinch of salt. Set aside.

Mix together the yogurt, Kashmiri chilli powder, garam masala, dried fenugreek, mustard oil and another pinch of salt. Pour over the chicken pieces and rub thoroughly until well coated. Cover and refrigerate for at least 3–4 hours.

When ready to cook, heat the oil in a saucepan over a medium heat. Add the tomatoes, ginger, garlic, green chillies, green cardamom pods, mace, cumin seeds and bay leaves to the pan, and sauté for a couple of minutes. Next, add the Kashmiri chilli powder and simmer over a medium heat for 20 minutes, or until the tomatoes are completely cooked.

Strain the sauce through a conical strainer or sieve and set the resulting liquid aside. Pour what is leftover in the sieve onto a tray and pick through to remove the whole spices. Transfer to a blender and blitz (with a little water, if required). Pass this through a sieve and add to the tomato sauce. Place the sauce back on the heat and cook for another 10–15 minutes. Check the seasoning, and finish with honey, cream, butter and dried fenugreek.

Meanwhile, grill the marinated chicken in a tandoor, or on a baking sheet in the oven at 200°C/180°C fan/400°F/Gas 6 for about 15–20 minutes, or until cooked through.

Put the cooked chicken pieces into a saucepan set over a medium heat and add the makhani sauce. Cook for another couple of minutes to reduce according to your desired consistency.

Serve with a blob of butter on top, with rice or naan.

DAL MAKHANI

This sumptuous North Indian dish of lentils slow-cooked with spices, butter and cream is traditionally prepared over a wood/coal fire for several hours. In my restaurants, we slowly cook the dal over a charcoal *tandoor*, which yields a thick, glorious-tasting dal. I also swap out the traditional kidney beans for chana dal, for a creamier texture. Making a good dal makhani is easy and requires only a few ingredients, but it does take time, so this is a great dish to make for a weekend or special festive meal. *Pictured overleaf (right)*.

Serves 4

DAL
200g/7oz/1¼ cups urad dal (whole black lentils)
50g/1¾oz/⅓ cup chana dal (split yellow lentils)
1 tsp salt
750ml/26fl oz/3¼ cups water

MASALA
2 tbsp ghee
3 tbsp salted butter
2 tsp Ginger-Garlic Paste (see page 17)
1 tsp Kashmiri chilli powder
½ tsp chilli powder
1 tbsp ground coriander
1 tsp salt, or more to taste
150g/5oz tomato purée/passata
50g/1¾oz tomato paste/tomato concentrate
150ml/5fl oz/⅔ cup water, plus extra as needed
4 tbsp double/heavy cream, plus extra to garnish
½ tsp Garam Masala (store-bought or see page 12)
2 tbsp dried fenugreek leaves

Wash the lentils well, then drain and place in a large bowl. Cover with fresh water and leave to soak overnight.

The next day, drain the lentils and transfer to a pressure cooker. Add the salt and measured water and pressure-cook on medium-high heat for 10 whistles. Reduce the heat to low-medium and cook for another 10 minutes (15–20 whistles). Let the pressure release naturally. You should be able to mash the lentils with your fingers. (If you don't have a pressure cooker, use a heavy pan, bring to the boil and simmer for 1 hour 30 minutes, or until soft.)

Mash some of the lentils with a potato masher, then reduce the heat to its lowest level and let the dal simmer while you make the masala.

In a large pan, heat the ghee and 2 tablespoons of the butter over a medium heat. Once melted, add the ginger-garlic paste and cook for 5 minutes until the raw smell goes away. Add the chilli powders, ground coriander and salt, stir well and cook for another minute or so. Stir in the tomato purée and cook for 2–4 minutes, or until well incorporated, then add the tomato paste and cook for another couple of minutes until you start to see oil oozing out from the sides.

Add the simmered dal and mix well, then stir in the measured water. Simmer over a low heat, uncovered, for around 45 minutes, stirring every 10 minutes or so and adding extra water as needed if it starts to look dry.

Add the remaining tablespoon of butter along with the cream and mix well. Simmer for a further 10 minutes, then add the garam masala and fenugreek. Taste for seasoning.

Serve hot with garlic naan or chapati, garnished with cream.

MOOLI PARATHA

These radish-stuffed wholemeal/wholewheat flatbreads are a family favourite. Parathas are very popular in North India – in the Punjab, they particularly like to eat them for breakfast. My mother used to make them with different fillings and we loved to eat them with butter, yogurt or pickles. They can be challenging to make at first, because mooli has a high water content – if you haven't removed enough moisture from your stuffing, rolling out can be difficult. With practice, you will soon get the hang of it. *Pictured overleaf (left).*

Serves 4–5

DOUGH
250g/9oz/2 cups wholemeal/wholewheat or multigrain flour
2 tsp rapeseed/canola oil, plus extra for greasing and cooking
3 tbsp water, or as needed

STUFFING
1 large mooli/white radish
¼ tsp salt, plus extra to taste
1 green chilli, finely chopped
2 tbsp finely chopped fresh coriander/cilantro
1 tbsp chopped fresh root ginger
1 tsp roasted ground cumin
½ tsp Garam Masala (store-bought or see page 12)

In a large bowl, combine the flour and 2 teaspoons of oil. Start adding water very slowly, mixing until a dough comes together. Knead for about 6–8 minutes to form a smooth ball of dough. Cover with a thin coating of oil and place it back in the bowl. Cover with a damp cloth and leave to rest for 15–20 minutes.

Peel the mooli and grate it straight into a bowl with a coarse box grater. Sprinkle with the salt and set aside for 15 minutes.

After this time, the mooli will have released a lot of water. Drain and squeeze the grated mooli to get rid of as much additional moisture as you can. Transfer the mooli to another bowl. Add the remaining stuffing ingredients and mix well. Do not add any extra salt at this point.

Heat a tawa (griddle) or large frying pan over a medium heat.

Divide the dough into 4–5 balls of equal size. Take one of the dough balls and use a rolling pin to roll it into a round disc, about 8–10cm/3–4in in diameter. Brush all over with a little oil. Place around 2 tablespoons of the mooli stuffing in the middle of the disc. Sprinkle with a little salt, then bring all the sides together to cover the filling and pinch to seal the edges. Flatten the resulting ball with your hands, then roll out with a rolling pin to a disc, 18–20cm/7–8in in diameter.

Transfer the rolled paratha to the hot tawa/pan. Cook on the first side for a minute or two, then flip. Apply a little oil to the top of the paratha and flip again. Now apply oil to the other side. Press down on the paratha with a spatula and cook, turning as needed, until both sides have golden brown spots.

Repeat to roll and cook the remaining paratha.

Serve with pickles or yogurt.

PALAK PANEER

One of my kids' favourites, we usually make *palak paneer* at home at least once a week. It makes a simply delicious, creamy and healthier side dish. If you prefer a milder gravy, you can leave out or reduce the green chillies. The cream is optional, but will give a more velvety texture to the dish.

Serves 4

500g/1lb 2oz spinach, leaves only (if using baby spinach, keep the stems), washed well and drained
50ml/3 tbsp plus 1 tsp cooking oil
1 tsp cumin seeds
180g/6½oz onions, finely chopped
1 tbsp Ginger-Garlic Paste (see page 17)
100g/3½oz tomatoes, chopped
2 green chillies (deseeded, if wished), chopped
1 tbsp dried fenugreek leaves
1 tsp hot chilli powder
½ tsp Garam Masala (store-bought or see page 12)
500g/1lb 2oz paneer
3 tbsp double/heavy cream (optional)
salt, to taste
2 tbsp julienned fresh root ginger, to garnish

Blanch the spinach in a large pan of water with ¼ teaspoon salt for 2 minutes. Drain and immerse in ice-cold water to stop the cooking, then drain again thoroughly.

Transfer half of the spinach to a blender and blitz to a smooth purée (you may need to add a splash of water to achieve this). Roughly chop the remaining spinach. Set both aside.

Heat the oil in a large pan over a medium heat. Add the cumin seeds and, once they start to crackle, add the onions and fry until golden. Add the ginger-garlic paste and cook for 1–2 minutes, or until it begins to smell aromatic, then add the tomatoes with a pinch of salt. Sauté until the tomatoes break down and turn mushy.

Add the green chillies, fenugreek, chilli powder and garam masala, and sauté for another 5–6 minutes until the masala is aromatic. Add a little water, if the pan is at all dry, cover with a lid and cook until the onions are completely soft. There should be some water left in the pan.

Reduce the heat, mix in the chopped and puréed spinach, and simmer for a further 2–3 minutes. If the curry is too thick, you may add a few more tablespoons of hot water, but avoid overcooking.

Add the paneer and cream (if using), and mix well. Taste for seasoning. Serve, garnished with julienned ginger with rice, chapati or naan.

MANGO LASSI

This yogurt-based drink is one of the most popular and traditional drinks in India. *Lassi* originated in the Punjab region and the word means "yogurt mixed with water" in Punjabi. Ideal for cooling you down in the hot summer, I have even seen the drink described as "the air conditioner of the Punjab"! There are so many variations: sweet, salty, flavoured... but I'm giving you a recipe for mango *lassi*, which is very popular in my restaurants. It's easy to make at home with a few simple ingredients. I love making mango *lassi*, especially during summer, when sweet mangoes are in season.

Serves 4

250g/9oz fresh mango pulp (from 2–3 sweet mangoes, or use canned mango pulp)
300g/10½oz/1¼ cups plain yogurt
2–3 tbsp sugar or sugar syrup
¼ tsp ground cardamom
chilled water or crushed ice, as needed
saffron strands and pistachios, to garnish (optional)

In a blender, combine the fresh mango pulp, yogurt, sugar or sugar syrup and ground cardamom. Add about 3 tablespoons of water or ice and blitz for around 60 seconds until everything is well combined. Check the sweetness and consistency, adding more sugar or water or ice, as desired, and blitz again.

Pour the lassi into chilled serving glasses, garnish with saffron strands and pistachio nuts (if wished), and serve chilled.

MOONG DAL HALWA

So easy to make at home with very few ingredients, this is a traditional dessert where ground yellow (moong) lentils are cooked in ghee over a slow heat until aromatic and golden, then flavoured with cardamom and saffron. Warming and filling, I prefer to eat this during the winter season.

Serves 4

150g/5oz/¾ cup moong dal
½ tsp saffron strands
50ml/3 tbsp plus 1 tsp lukewarm milk
150g/5oz ghee
100ml/3½fl oz/scant ½ cup water
100g/3½oz/½ cup granulated sugar
¼ tsp ground cardamom

TO DECORATE
10 almonds, chopped
5 pistachios, chopped

First, soak the moong dal for about 2 hours, then drain and transfer to a blender. Grind until smooth, then set aside.

In a small bowl, soak the saffron strands in the lukewarm milk and set aside.

Heat the ghee in a heavy pan over a low heat. Once melted, add the ground lentils and cook until golden brown and crumbly.

In a separate pan, combine the measured water and sugar. Bring to the boil until the sugar has melted and you have a thick syrup.

Mix the moong dal batter into the sugar syrup along with the saffron milk, stirring constantly. The mixture will become runny at this stage, but will thicken within a few minutes. Keep over a low heat, stirring constantly, until the moisture evaporates.

Reduce the heat to as low as possible, add the ground cardamom and keep stirring and breaking up any lumps in the mixture until the halwa turns deeply golden and aromatic.

Remove from the heat and divide among bowls. Decorate with chopped almonds and pistachios, and serve hot.

UTTAR PRADESH

UTTAR PRADESH

The region of Uttar Pradesh in northern India is the country's fourth largest in land area and the most populated. With the Himalayas bordering the state to the north, its landscape is a varied one of hills, plains, valleys and plateaus, and its temperate climate means that it is an important centre for agriculture, producing staples such as wheat, rice, potatoes, pulses and sugar cane.

The food of the region, which you will often see referred to as Awadhi cuisine, is just as diverse as its geography. Heavily influenced by the Muslim cuisines of the Mughlai Empire, richly spiced meat dishes are common. The royal kitchens of the Nawabs (the ruling nobility of the 18th and 19th centuries) produced many famous dishes, which are still enjoyed throughout the region today. By their very nature as extravagant royal delicacies, many take several hours to prepare, but they are always worth taking time over as the flavours are outstanding.

The region's capital city of Lucknow (formerly named Awadh, which is where the term Awadhi cuisine stems from) is a culinary centre, famous for its various meat kebabs (see pages 48 and 50), rich *Nihari* lamb stew (page 61) and biryanis (page 62). Among the vegetarian classics of the region are numerous *subzis* (vegetable stir-fries), including the breakfast dish of *Poori Subzi* (page 53), a simple but hearty potato curry served with flaky fried breads, and the celebratory *Navaratan Korma* (page 56), which features no less than nine varieties of colourful vegetables in a mild, creamy sauce.

SHAMI KEBAB

Shami kebab is a popular street-food snack, usually made with chicken, lamb or beef, but here I have chosen to use goat meat, which is an economical option and just as succulent and tasty. It is such a widespread dish in northern India that you will find every person has their own way of making it. The chopped herbs and red onions in my version give it a nice chunky texture and you get a little bit of sweetness coming through from the onions.

Serves 4–5

75g/2½oz/generous ¾ cup chana dal (yellow split peas), rinsed and drained
3 tbsp cooking oil, plus extra for deep-frying
4–5 cloves
4 green cardamom pods
2 bay leaves
1 tsp black peppercorns
30g/1oz fresh root ginger, roughly chopped
5–6 garlic cloves, crushed
500g/1lb 2oz boneless goat meat (or lamb or beef), cut into 2.5cm/1in chunks
1 tbsp ground coriander
1 tsp Kashmiri chilli powder
1 tsp ground cumin
½ tsp ground turmeric
1 tsp salt, or to taste
300ml/10½fl oz/1¼ cups water
1 egg
5 tbsp finely chopped fresh coriander/cilantro stems
2 tbsp finely chopped fresh mint
4 tbsp finely chopped red onion (optional)
4 tbsp cornflour/cornstarch
4 green chillies, chopped
1 tsp seeds from black cardamom pods
Mint and Coriander Chutney (see page 18), to serve

Soak the chana dal in a bowl of hot water for 20–30 minutes, then drain.

Heat the oil in a large pan (that has a lid) over a medium heat. Add all of the whole spices, then when they start crackling, add the ginger and garlic, and sauté for 4–5 minutes. Add the meat and sauté until you see juice coming out from the meat, then add the ground spices and salt. Mix well and cook for 10–15 minutes.

Add the measured water and cook for 15–20 minutes, then add the soaked chana dal, cover and reduce the heat to low. Cook for about 20–25 minutes until the meat is fully cooked.

Leave to cool, then remove all the whole spices from the mixture.

Put the cooled mixture through a mincer at least twice, or blitz in a food processor, until finely ground. Place in a bowl, add the remaining ingredients and mix well. Divide the mixture into 10–12 balls of equal size, then flatten them into patties.

Heat enough oil for deep-frying in a large heavy pan or deep-fat fryer to 180°C/350°F. Add the patties, in batches, and deep-fry for 6–8 minutes until golden brown. Remove with a slotted spoon to a plate lined with paper towels.

Serve hot with Mint and Coriander Chutney (see page 18), lemon wedges, fresh coriander and sliced onion.

TUNDAY KABAB

These melt-in-the-mouth lamb patties are from the historic city of Lucknow, famous for its succulent kebabs. The raw papaya paste is used as a meat tenderizer – it is available in Indian grocery stores. If you can't find it, use pineapple juice instead. An optional step here is to smoke the lamb before cooking, which makes the meat delightfully aromatic.

Serves 4

500g/1lb 2oz very finely minced/ground lamb
2 tbsp raw papaya paste (or pineapple juice)
2 tbsp gram flour/besan
100g/3½oz ghee, for frying
50g/1¾oz onions, finely chopped
2–3 saffron strands
2 tbsp milk
1 tbsp Ginger-Garlic Paste (see page 17)
2 tbsp Kashmiri chilli powder
1½ tsp rose water
2 tbsp dried rose petals
1–1½ tsp salt, to taste

SPICE MIX

2.5cm/1in cinnamon stick
6 cloves
4 black cardamom pods
4 green cardamom pods
pinch of freshly grated nutmeg
½ blade of mace
1 tbsp poppy seeds
1 tsp cumin seeds
½ tsp mustard seeds
2 bay leaves

SMOKY INFUSION (OPTIONAL)

1 piece of charcoal
¼ tsp ghee
3 cloves
3 green cardamom pods

Place the lamb in a bowl along with the raw papaya paste and mix well. Leave at room temperature for 2 hours. This will tenderize the meat.

Roast the gram flour in a dry frying pan over a low heat until fragrant. Remove from the heat and set aside.

In the same pan, dry-roast the spices for the spice mix. Let cool, then grind to a fine powder in a spice grinder.

Heat 1–2 tablespoons of the ghee in the same pan over a medium heat and sauté the onions until golden brown. Let cool, then grind to a fine paste. Set aside.

Soak the saffron strands in the milk for 15–20 minutes.

Add the roasted gram flour, spice mix, onion paste and saffron milk to the lamb along with the ginger-garlic paste, chilli powder, rose water, dried rose petals and salt. Mix thoroughly, then cover and refrigerate for 4–5 hours.

If you want to infuse the meat with smoky flavour, remove the bowl of marinated lamb from the refrigerator. Light a small piece of charcoal, place it in a small heatproof metal bowl and nestle it into the bowl containing the meat. Pour the ghee on top of the coal, and sprinkle over the cloves and cardamom pods. Quickly cover the large bowl with foil and set aside to smoke for about 20 minutes.

Divide the meat into 12–16 small balls and flatten into patties. Heat the remaining ghee in a large frying pan and fry the patties over a very low heat, turning regularly, until cooked through.

Serve with paratha, sliced onions, lemon wedges and Mint and Coriander Chutney (see page 18).

CHICKEN TIKKA MIRZA HUSNOO

This recipe, which come from the royal kitchens of Lucknow (and was named for a former *nizam*), produces succulent, lightly spiced morsels of chicken coated in an indulgent saffron cream sauce. It takes only 10 minutes to cook, but plan ahead as it takes 2½ hours to marinate. It is well worth the time. Serve with Mint and Coriander Chutney (page 18).

Serves 4

1kg/2lb 4oz boneless chicken thighs, trimmed and halved
100g/3½oz butter, melted
½ tsp saffron strands mixed with 4 tbsp double/heavy cream
a pinch of each, to serve:
  dried mango powder/amchur, black rock salt powder, ground fenugreek, ground cinnamon, ground cloves, ground mace

FIRST MARINADE

2 tbsp Garlic-Ginger Paste (see page 17)
4 tsp white pepper
4 tbsp malt vinegar
1 tbsp salt, or to taste

MASALA

2 tbsp mustard oil
1 tbsp salted butter
1 tsp black cumin seeds
8 garlic cloves, chopped
2 tbsp gram flour/besan

SECOND MARINADE

200g/7oz/generous ¾ cup plain yogurt
30g/1oz soft cream cheese
4 tbsp double/heavy cream
4 tsp Ginger-Garlic Paste (see page 17)
¾ tsp ground white pepper
4 green chillies, chopped
1 tbsp ground coriander

In a large bowl, combine all the ingredients for the first marinade. Add the chicken pieces, mix well to coat, cover and set aside at room temperature for 30 minutes.

Next, make the masala. In a frying pan, heat the mustard oil to smoking point, then remove from the heat and let cool to room temperature. Add the butter and put the pan back over a medium heat, then add the black cumin seeds and stir until they begin to crackle. Add the garlic and stir-fry until golden. Finally, add the gram flour and stir-fry until it smells nutty. Remove from the heat and leave to cool.

Rub the masala into the chicken pieces and set aside for another 30 minutes.

In a separate bowl, combine all the ingredients for the second marinade. Rub it into the chicken pieces, cover and set aside for 1 hour.

Preheat the oven to 180°C/160°C fan/350°F/Gas 4 (or get a barbecue hot).

Thread the chicken pieces onto 6–8 metal skewers. Bake for 10–15 minutes, then remove from the oven and baste with the melted butter, then return to the oven for a further 2–3 minutes. (Alternatively, cook over the barbecue, turning and basting as needed.)

Place the skewers on a platter, brush with the saffron cream and sprinkle over a pinch of each of the ground spices. Serve with onion rings, green chillies and lemon wedges.

POORI SUBZI

This is a popular breakfast dish in India – a light, fragrant curry of spicy, softly mashed potatoes served with crusty, deep-fried bread. It's a common preparation across the country and every region has their own recipe – this one has flavours from the north, with cumin seeds and yogurt featuring.

Serves 4

POORI
250g/9oz/1⅔ cups wholemeal/ wholewheat or multigrain flour
50g/1¾oz/generous ⅓ cup semolina
a pinch of salt
2 tbsp rapeseed/canola oil, plus extra for deep-frying
60–80ml/2–3fl oz/ 4–5 tbsp water

SUBZI
2 tbsp rapeseed/canola oil
1 tsp cumin seeds
1 green chilli, deseeded and finely chopped
1 medium tomato, roughly chopped
1 tsp hot chilli powder
¼ tsp ground turmeric
2 tsp ground coriander
250g/9oz potatoes, boiled, peeled and cubed
100g/3½oz/generous ⅓ cup plain yogurt
240ml/9fl oz/1 cup water, plus 4 tbsp
½ tsp Garam Masala (store-bought or see page 12)
5–6 sprigs of fresh coriander/ cilantro, finely chopped
salt, to taste

First, prepare the poori. Put the flour and semolina into a bowl. Add the salt, rapeseed oil and enough of the measured water to bring everything together. Knead to a stiff dough. Cover with a cloth and set aside for 15–20 minutes.

Heat the oil for the subzi in a non-stick pan over a medium heat. Add the cumin seeds and let crackle, then add the green chilli and tomato. Sauté until the tomato breaks down and becomes mushy. Stir in the chilli powder, turmeric and ground coriander, and sauté over a low heat for 6–8 minutes. Check the consistency – if it's too thick, add 3–4 tablespoons of water. Cook for a further 1–2 minutes.

Gently mix in the potato cubes and yogurt. Season with salt to taste and gently mix again. Add the measured water and cook over a low heat for a further 4–5 minutes, stirring occasionally, until thickened.

Divide the poori dough into 8–10 equal portions, then gently roll each piece between your palms and shape into balls.

Heat enough oil for deep-frying in a deep, heavy pan or deep-fat fryer to 170°C/340°F.

Slightly flatten each ball of dough with your palm, then use a rolling pin to roll out into 8–10cm/3–4in discs. Deep-fry the discs in the hot oil until they puff up and turn light golden brown, about 2–3 minutes. Drain on paper towels.

Lightly mash the potato cubes in the curry and add another 4 tablespoons of water. Bring to the boil, then stir in the garam masala and fresh coriander, reserving some for garnish. Remove from the heat.

Put the fried pooris into a serving bowl and the potato subzi into another. Garnish with the remaining coriander and serve hot.

NARGISI KOFTA

This dish was on my very first menu for the opening of my restaurant Kutir. Spiced mutton keema wrapped around hard-boiled eggs (the Indian version of Scotch eggs) braised in a luxurious gravy. It takes time to make, but you must try it as it really is unique. Serve with pulao, biryani or roti/parathas (I prefer parathas, as my mother used to make them for us).

Serves 4

350g/12oz minced/ground mutton
¼ tsp ground nutmeg
4 tbsp Ginger-Garlic Paste (see page 17)
1½ tsp Kashmiri chilli powder
1 tsp ground coriander
1 tsp ground turmeric
1 tsp Garam Masala (store-bought or see page 12)
2 tbsp finely chopped fresh mint
2 tbsp cornflour/cornstarch
2 tbsp mustard oil
4 eggs, hard-boiled and peeled
salt, to taste

GRAVY

100ml/3½fl oz/scant ½ cup rapeseed/canola oil
2 dried red chillies
2 black cardamom pods
4 cloves
2.5cm/1in cinnamon stick
1 bay leaf
150g/5oz onion, chopped
2 tsp Ginger-Garlic Paste (see page 17)
1 tbsp chopped green chillies
50g/1¾oz tomato purée/tomato concentrate
1 tbsp ground coriander
1 tsp ground cumin
1 tsp Kashmiri chilli powder
½ tsp ground turmeric
150g/5oz/⅔ cup plain yogurt
250ml/9fl oz/1 cup water
1 tsp Garam Masala (store-bought or see page 12)
1 tsp dried fenugreek leaves

In a food processor, thoroughly blitz the minced mutton together with the nutmeg to make it soft and tender. Alternatively, put it through a meat mincer twice.

Place the mutton in a bowl, add the ginger-garlic paste, ground spices, mint, cornflour and 1 teaspoon of salt. Mix well using your hands. Divide the mixture into 4 parts. Put ½ tablespoon of mustard oil in your palm, take one portion of the meat mixture and pat it out to form a flat disc, about the size of a chapati. Place a hard-boiled egg on top, then wrap the meat mixture around it to enclose. Repeat with the rest of the meat mixture and eggs. Set aside.

Heat the oil for the gravy in a large pan (that has a lid) over a medium heat. Add the whole spices and bay leaf and sauté for a minute (I personally prefer to use whole spices for meat preparations – they greatly benefit the final flavour). Next, add the chopped onion and sauté until lightly browned. Add the ginger-garlic paste and green chillies and sauté a little, then add the tomato purée, ground coriander, cumin, chilli powder and turmeric. Sauté until the oil separates from the mixture.

Whisk a pinch of salt into the yogurt, then add to the gravy. Mix well, then add the measured water and bring to the boil. Gently nestle the meat-wrapped eggs into the gravy, reduce to a simmer, then cover and cook for 15–20 minutes.

Check the seasoning, then add the garam masala and dried fenugreek leaves. Serve hot.

NAVARATAN KORMA

This is a mildly sweet vegetarian korma from the royal kitchens of Lucknow, with an exciting combination of mixed vegetables in a creamy, nutty sauce. *Navaratan* means nine ingredients – traditionally all colourful vegetables. I've included sultanas (golden raisins), and paneer because it's a firm favourite of vegetarians. *Pictured overleaf (right).*

Serves 4

10–12 blanched almonds
10–12 cashews
1 tbsp poppy seeds
1 tbsp melon seeds
4 tbsp water, or as needed
100ml/3½fl oz/scant ½ cup rapeseed/canola oil
2–3 green cardamom pods
1 black cardamom pod
3 cloves
2.5cm/1in cinnamon stick
2 bay leaves
2 blades of mace
250g/9oz onions, thinly sliced
1 tbsp Ginger-Garlic paste (see page 17)
1 tbsp finely chopped green chillies
100g/3½oz/generous ⅓ cup plain yogurt
½ tsp ground turmeric
1 tsp Kashmiri chilli powder
70g/2½oz carrots, diced
50g/1¾oz fresh or frozen peas
150g/5oz potatoes, diced
50g/1¾oz green beans, cut into small batons
100g/3½oz small cauliflower florets
1 tbsp sultanas/golden raisins
100g/3½oz paneer, cubed
3 tbsp double/heavy cream
½ tsp Garam Masala (store-bought or see page 12)
handful of crispy fried onions
1 tbsp chopped fresh mint leaves
salt, to taste

Soak the blanched almonds, cashews, poppy and melon seeds in hot water for 30–40 minutes. Drain, then transfer to a pestle and mortar or spice grinder. Add 4 tablespoons of water and grind to a smooth, fine paste, adding more water if needed. Set aside.

Heat the oil in a large, heavy pan (that has a lid) over a medium heat. Add the whole spices and sauté until they crackle, then add the sliced onions and sauté until golden. Add the ginger-garlic paste and chopped green chillies and sauté for a minute, then reduce the heat to very low and add the nut-seed paste and yogurt, stirring vigorously to combine. Add the turmeric and chilli powder and sauté for 3–4 minutes over a low heat, stirring often.

Add the carrots, peas, potatoes, green beans, cauliflower, sultanas and paneer, and stir well. Add 250ml/9fl oz/1 cup water, season with salt, cover and simmer until the vegetables are fork-tender.

To finish, add the cream and stir to combine, then remove from the heat and sprinkle over the garam masala. Garnish with fried onions and fresh mint leaves, and serve with chapati or tandoori parathas.

SHEERMAL

Another famous recipe from the royal family of Lucknow, this saffron-infused bread is sweet and luxurious. You will often find it for sale in local restaurants and hotels in northern India. Soft and fluffy, it makes a perfect companion to rich curries, like *Nihari* (page 61), or kebabs, or even a delightful treat on its own. *Pictured overleaf (left).*

Makes 8

250ml/9fl oz/1 cup warm milk
1 tsp saffron strands
2 tsp granulated sugar
½ tsp ground cardamom
300g/10½oz/scant 2½ cups plain/all-purpose flour
1 tsp salt
115g/3¾oz ghee, melted, plus 1–2 tsp for brushing

Place 3 tablespoons of the milk in a small bowl and dissolve the saffron in it. Set aside.

Dissolve the sugar and cardamom in the remaining milk.

In a large bowl, combine the flour and salt. Make a well in the middle and pour in the milk-sugar mixture, 2 teaspoons of the saffron milk (reserve the rest) and the melted ghee. Start mixing gradually, then knead to a soft dough. Cover with a damp cloth and set aside for 10–15 minutes.

Divide the dough into 8 equal-sized portions. Shape them into balls, then cover with a damp cloth and set aside for a further 10–15 minutes.

Preheat the oven to 180°C/160°C fan/350°F/Gas 4. Grease a baking sheet with a little ghee or line with baking paper.

Working with one ball at a time, roll out to a disc, about 13cm/5in in diameter. These should not be rolled out thinly. Prick the entire surface of each disc with a fork and transfer to the prepared baking sheet.

Bake the flatbreads for 5 minutes, then remove from the oven and brush the surface of the breads with the remaining saffron-infused milk. Bake for a further 6–7 minutes, or until the breads are golden.

Brush with ghee as soon as you take the breads out of the oven and serve warm.

NIHARI

Nihari is a sumptuous meat stew, carefully prepared with a unique blend of spices, and traditionally associated with the royal cuisine of Uttar Pradesh. It requires a considerable amount of time to cook – around 5 hours – which makes it a natural choice for celebratory meals such as Eid dinners and other joyous occasions. It is usually cooked with either mutton or goat meat, but it can also be made with chicken or beef. I prefer to use lamb shanks or any meat on the bone, which will add richness to the gravy.

Serves 4

- 3 tbsp ghee or vegetable oil
- 2 medium onions, finely sliced
- 4 lamb shanks
- 2 tbsp Ginger-Garlic Paste (see page 17)
- 2 tsp ground coriander
- 2 tbsp hot chilli powder
- ½ tsp ground turmeric
- 2 tbsp nihari masala (see below)
- 240ml/8fl oz/1 cup water
- 2 tbsp gram flour/besan, toasted over a low heat
- 1 tbsp fresh lime juice
- 2 tbsp julienned fresh root ginger
- 4 tbsp chopped fresh coriander/cilantro leaves
- salt, to taste

NIHARI MASALA

- 100g/3½oz cloves
- 50g/1¾oz black cardamom pods
- 2 whole nutmegs

To make the nihari masala, dry-roast the whole spices, then grind to a powder in a spice grinder. Store in an airtight jar.

In a deep, heavy pan, heat the ghee or oil (ghee makes the dish more flavourful, so do use it if possible). When hot, toss in the sliced onions and fry over a medium heat until golden brown. Add the lamb shanks, ginger-garlic paste, ground coriander, red chilli powder and ground turmeric with a dash of salt. Mix well to coat the meat in the ghee and seasonings, then sauté over a high heat for 8–10 minutes.

Add your prepared nihari spice powder along with about 120ml/4fl oz/½ cup water. Cover and simmer over a low heat for about 1½ hours, or until cooked. You will know the dish is ready when the meat falls apart when pressed with a wooden spoon.

Combine the gram flour with 120ml/4fl oz/½ cup water and stir until there are no more lumps, then add it to the sauce. Stir thoroughly to combine and simmer for a further 10–15 minutes until the sauce has thickened.

To complete the dish, add the lime juice, ginger and freshly chopped coriander. Serve hot with flatbreads and/or rice.

CHICKEN BIRYANI

Is there anything as satisfying as an aromatic, fluffy biryani, fresh from the pot? Biryani hails from the Mughlai cuisine and there are many variations on it, influenced by the wide regions through which the Mughals travelled. This is a typical Lucknowi (or Awadhi) biryani, ideal for a special occasion.

Serves 4

500g/17½oz/2½ cups basmati rice, rinsed and drained
500g/1lb 2oz skinless boneless chicken, cut into bite-size pieces
100ml/3½fl oz/scant ½ cup rapeseed/canola oil, plus 1 tbsp
2 bay leaves
1 cinnamon stick
4 cloves
4 whole black peppercorns
2 green cardamom pods
2 black cardamom pods
1 star anise
1 blade of mace
3 onions, finely sliced
3 tbsp Ginger-Garlic Paste (see page 17)
5 green chillies, slit
12g/½oz/¼ cup fresh coriander/cilantro leaves
12g/½oz/¼ cup fresh mint leaves
2 tbsp lemon juice
3 tbsp ghee, melted
a few saffron strands soaked in 1 tsp milk
1 tbsp kewra water (or rose water)
1 tbsp single/light cream
4 tbsp fried onions
salt, to taste

MARINADE
180g/6½oz/¾ cup plain yogurt
juice of 1 lemon
2 tsp Kashmiri chilli powder
½ tsp ground turmeric
2 tbsp ground coriander
2 tsp salt

Place the rice in a large bowl of water and leave to soak.

Combine all the marinade ingredients in a large bowl. Add the chicken, mix well and leave to marinate for about 45 minutes.

Heat the oil in a large pan (that has a lid) over a medium heat. Add the bay leaves, cinnamon, cloves, black peppercorns, cardamom pods, star anise and mace. Once they start to crackle, add the onions and fry until golden brown. Add the ginger-garlic paste and fry until the raw smell goes away, then add the chillies and half of the coriander and mint leaves. Sauté for a couple of minutes. Once the oil starts separating, add the chicken along with its marinade and stir well. Increase the heat to high and cook for 8–10 minutes, stirring continuously. Taste and adjust the salt and spices to suit. Cover, reduce the heat to low and cook for 10–15 minutes.

Drain the rice. Fill a large pan with double the quantity of fresh water as there is rice, then add a few drops of lemon juice and a tablespoon of oil. Bring to the boil, then add the drained rice along with a pinch of salt. Boil for 8–10 minutes, or until the rice is almost cooked. Drain well, then spread the rice over a tray to separate the grains.

Set a separate heavy pan over a medium heat. Evenly spread half of the chicken mixture over the base of the pan, then evenly spread half of the rice on top. Sprinkle over a spoonful of ghee, half of the saffron milk and half of the remaining coriander and mint. Repeat this layering again (reserving a few sprigs of the herbs for garnish) and additionally sprinkling over the remaining lemon juice, kewra water, cream and fried onions. Seal the pan tightly with aluminium foil and cover it with the lid. Let it cook over a low heat for 10–15 minutes.

Remove the foil from one side and mix the biryani well (do this carefully so the rice grains don't break). Serve garnished with the remaining herbs, with raita on the side.

DUM KA MURGH

This slow-cooked chicken in a cashew-nut and poppy-seed gravy is another popular curry dish from the royal kitchens. The chicken is first marinated in yogurt and spices, then simmered slowly in its marinade, which gives a rich colour and texture to the gravy. Serve with roti or naan.

Serves 4

1kg/2lb 4oz boneless chicken thighs, trimmed and halved
150ml/5fl oz/⅔ cup rapeseed/canola oil or ghee
200g/7oz onions, thinly sliced
2 tsp Ginger-Garlic Paste (see page 17)
50g/1¾oz poppy seeds, soaked in water for 15–20 minutes
100g/3½oz cashews, fried until golden, plus extra to serve
3 green chillies, deseeded and chopped
2 tbsp chopped coriander/cilantro
2 tbsp chopped fresh mint leaves

MARINADE

150g/5oz/⅔ cup plain yogurt
½ tsp ground turmeric
2 tsp Kashmiri chilli powder
1 tbsp ground coriander
2 tbsp mustard oil
1 tsp lemon juice
1 tsp salt
1 tbsp dried rose petals
1 tbsp kewra water (optional)
1 tsp Ginger-Garlic Paste (see page 17)

WHOLE SPICES

2 bay leaves
4 green cardamom pods
2 black cardamom pods
2.5cm/1in cinnamon stick
1 tsp mace
4 cloves
4 black peppercorns
½ tsp salt in 3 tbsp water

In a large bowl, combine all the ingredients for the marinade. Add the chicken, mix well, then cover and refrigerate for 2–3 hours.

Heat the oil or ghee in a large, heavy pan (that has a lid) over a medium heat. Add all the whole spices along with the salty water and let them crackle (the salty water helps to release the flavours from the whole spices). After a few seconds, remove all the whole spices from the oil with a slotted spoon. Add the sliced onions to the pan and sauté until golden brown. Add the ginger-garlic paste and sauté briefly, then add the chicken with its marinade. Increase the heat to high and bring to the boil. Cook until the sauce starts to reduce, then lower to a simmer, cover and cook for a further 20–30 minutes.

Put the soaked and drained poppy seeds, fried cashews and green chillies in a pestle and mortar or spice grinder and grind to a smooth, fine paste. Add the paste to the curry and mix well. Taste to adjust the salt and add a little water, if needed, to bring the sauce consistency to your liking. Cover once again and cook for a final 7–8 minutes.

Serve garnished with more fried cashews, fresh coriander and mint.

FISH SALAN

This home-style fish curry is from the small villages of Uttar Pradesh. Most villagers make it with local fish and very limited ingredients. You can blend the spice paste in a pestle and mortar, as they would have done it traditionally, but these days a high-speed food processor will do the job in minutes. This is a very simple and easy to make recipe.

Serves 4

500g/1lb 2oz cod, stone bass or other white fish, cut into about 8 large chunks
100ml/3½fl oz/scant ½ cup rapeseed/canola oil, plus 2 tbsp
1 tsp fenugreek seeds
1 tsp cumin seeds
2 dried red chillies
100ml/3½fl oz/scant ½ cup water, or as needed
fresh coriander/cilantro leaves, to garnish

MARINADE
1 tsp white vinegar
½ tsp garlic paste
½ tsp Kashmiri chilli powder
2 tbsp gram flour/besan
1 tbsp rice flour
1 tbsp finely chopped green chilli
1 tbsp finely chopped fresh root ginger
¼ tsp Garam Masala (store-bought or see page 12)
pinch of salt

CURRY PASTE
100g/3½oz onion, chopped
150g/5oz tomatoes, chopped
1 tsp Ginger-Garlic Paste (see page 17)
1 tsp Kashmiri chilli powder
1 tsp ground coriander
½ tsp ground turmeric
½ tsp Garam Masala (store-bought or see page 12)
1 tbsp plain yogurt
pinch of salt

In a large bowl, mix all the ingredients for the marinade. Add the fish pieces and mix to combine. Leave to marinate for 30 minutes.

Heat the 100ml/3½fl oz/scant ½ cup rapeseed oil in a deep pan over a medium-high heat. Add the marinated fish pieces in small batches and fry until crisp. Remove and set aside.

Put all the ingredients for the curry paste in a food processor and blitz to a fine paste.

Heat the 2 tablespoons of oil in a frying pan over a medium heat. Add the fenugreek seeds, cumin seeds and dried chillies, and sauté for 10–15 seconds, then add the curry paste and cook until the oil separates and the raw aroma of garlic and ginger goes away. Gently add the fish pieces along with the water, adjusting the thickness of the gravy to your liking. Cook for 2 minutes.

Garnish with coriander leaves and serve with rice.

SHAHI TUKDA

This rich and festive dessert is created with mostly humble ingredients – just bread, ghee, sugar and milk – but is made luxurious by the addition of saffron and nuts. It is a very popular classic royal dessert and is said to have originated during the Mughal region. *Shahi tukda* was a favourite of the Mughal emperors and was enjoyed with their festive *iftar* meals during the month of Ramadan.

Serves 4

pinch of saffron strands
2 tbsp warm milk
4 slices of slightly stale white bread (do not use brown bread or very soft bread, as it will absorb too much ghee when frying), crusts removed
2–3 tbsp ghee
30g/1oz/¼ cup slivered pistachios, toasted
30g/1oz/¼ cup whole almonds, toasted

REDUCED MILK

750ml/26fl oz/3¼ cups whole milk
100ml/3½fl oz/scant ½ cup condensed milk
4 tbsp granulated sugar
pinch of saffron strands

SUGAR SYRUP

150g/5oz/generous ⅔ cup granulated sugar
150ml/5fl oz/⅔ cup water
½ tsp rose water
½ tsp ground cardamom

Soak the saffron in the warm milk.

Cut the bread slices either in diagonally half or into quarter triangles. Set aside in a warm place to keep them dry.

To make the reduced milk, bring the milk to the boil in a wide pan, then reduce the heat to low and simmer until the milk has reduced by half (it will take 40–50 minutes – keep stirring so the milk does not stick to the bottom of the pan). Add the condensed milk, sugar and saffron, and simmer for another 5 minutes until thick. Leave to cool.

To make the sugar syrup, combine the sugar and measured water in a pan. Bring to the boil and keep boiling until you reach one-thread consistency. To test this, dip a wooden spoon into the syrup and let the mixture cool slightly until you can touch it. Touch your forefinger to the syrup, then bring your thumb and forefinger together and pull apart gently. If a single thread of syrup that does not break is formed, you have the right consistency. Remove from the heat and stir in the rose water and ground cardamom.

Heat the ghee in a frying pan over a low heat and fry the bread slices on both sides until golden and crispy.

Dip the fried bread slices in the sugar syrup until well coated, then place on a wire rack to let any excess syrup drain away. Divide among 4 serving plates. Just before serving, evenly pour the cooled reduced milk over the bread slices and decorate with toasted pistachios and almonds. Serve warm or chilled.

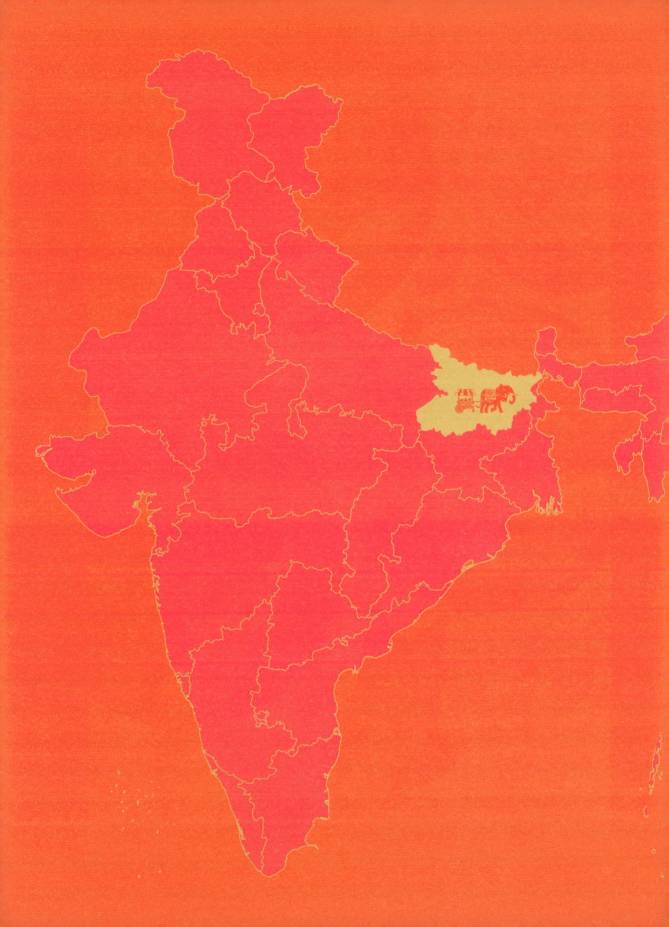

BIHAR

BIHAR

Bihar in eastern India – the land of the Bodhi tree where Buddha found enlightenment – is a vibrant region with a rich cultural and wholesome gastronomic heritage. Its food shares many similar characteristics with other northern and eastern Indian cuisines (including Nepalese and Bengali traditions). Dal is a staple food, and mustard oil and turmeric feature heavily. The food is hearty and straightforward, and tends to be milder in terms of spicing, tailored to those who spend long days farming or performing manual labour.

Bihar's most famous dish is *Litti Chokha* (see page 75) – baked wheat-flour cakes filled with roasted gram flour/besan and spices, which are served with *chokha*, a savoury mash made from potaoes, roasted aubergine/eggplant and tomatoes. *Chokha* is the name for numerous mashed vegetable preparations, which can be found throughout the region. *Dal Puri* (page 83), fried, lentil-stuffed breads, are also very popular.

There are numerous Bihari meat dishes, with chicken and mutton being the most common, whereas beef and pork are generally avoided. The region of Champaran is famous for its mutton curry (page 76). Fish dishes abound in the Mithila region of northern Bihar, due to the number of rivers that flow through the land there.

Festivals always feature *Laung Lata* (page 86). These are crispy fried pastry morsels filled with a sweet milk filling, dipped in sugar syrup and sealed with an aromatic clove, and are not to be missed.

JHALMURI

This is a popular and mouthwatering Bihari street snack. Traditionally served in a rolled cone of newspaper, it is a delicious savoury mix of puffed rice and Bombay mix with crunchy peanuts, fresh onions, cucumbers, tomatoes and green chillies.

Serves 4

DRY INGREDIENTS
600g/1lb 5oz/3 cups puffed rice
120g/4oz/1 cup Bombay mix
2 tbsp masala moong dal (ready-made mix available in Asian stores and some supermarkets)
2 tbsp spicy aloo bhujia (seasoned potato noodles, available in Asian stores and some supermarkets)
2 tbsp roasted chickpeas/garbanzo beans
2 tbsp roasted skinless peanuts
1 tbsp Chaat Masala (store-bought or see page 15)
½ tsp roasted ground cumin

FRESH INGREDIENTS
2 tbsp finely chopped red onion
2 tbsp chopped cucumber (deseed the cucumber first)
2 tbsp chopped fresh coriander/cilantro
1 tbsp chopped tomato (deseed the tomato first)
2 green chillies, finely chopped, to taste
1 tbsp chopped fresh root ginger
1 tbsp lime juice
2 tsp mustard oil

For *jhalmuri*, the puffed rice needs to be very crisp. If it is not crisp, you can dry it out in a hot pan, tossing it with a pinch of salt until all the moisture has evaporated. Set aside.

Thoroughly combine all the fresh ingredients in a large mixing bowl.

In a separate bowl, combine all the dry ingredients, then transfer them to the bowl of fresh ingredients and mix by hand until everything is very well combined.

Taste for seasoning – you may want to adjust the levels of salt, mustard oil or fresh chilli to suit your preference. If the mixture is too moist, you can add some more puffed rice or Bombay mix.

Serve immediately. You cannot keep *jhalmuri* for any length of time as it will become soggy.

LITTI CHOKHA

This is a typically Bihari dish of wholewheat dough balls stuffed with a spicy filling, served alongside *chokha*, a dish of spiced mashed potatoes, aubergine/eggplant and tomatoes. It is a popular evening snack, but filling enough to be a complete meal. Traditionally, the *litti* would be roasted over charcoal, but it is more convenient to fry or bake them.

Serves 6–7

DOUGH
240g/8½oz/generous 1½ cups wholemeal/wholewheat flour
¼ tsp salt
½ tsp carom seeds/ajwain
2 tbsp vegetable oil
300ml/10½fl oz/1¼ cups rapeseed/canola oil, for frying
2 tbsp hot melted ghee, to serve

STUFFING
125g/4oz/generous 1 cup roasted gram flour/besan
2 green chillies, finely chopped
1 tbsp finely chopped onion
1 tbsp chopped fresh root ginger
1 tbsp chopped garlic
2 tbsp chopped fresh coriander/cilantro
1 tsp dried mango powder/amchur
1 tsp lemon juice
½ tsp roasted cumin seeds
½ tsp carom seeds/ajwain
2 tsp mustard oil
salt, to taste

CHOKHA
1 large aubergine/eggplant
150g/5oz/¾ cup mashed potatoes
50g/1¾oz tomatoes, deseeded and chopped
2 green chillies, finely chopped
100g/3½oz onions, finely chopped
1 tbsp chopped coriander/cilantro
1 tbsp mustard oil
½ tsp toasted cumin seeds
1 tsp lime juice
salt, to taste

For the dough, sift the flour and salt into a large bowl and add the carom seeds and vegetable oil. Mix to combine, then add enough water to bring the mixture to a stiff dough. Knead well, then cover with a damp cloth and set aside while you make the stuffing.

Combine all the stuffing ingredients in a separate bowl and and mix well. If the stuffing looks a little dry, you can add a little water to bring it together, but don't make it too soft. Divide into 6–7 equal portions.

Divide the dough into 6–7 equal balls. Flatten each ball with your palm and make a depression in the middle. Fill with a portion of the stuffing and fold the sides of the dough over to enclose it. Flatten the balls a little with your palm.

Heat the oil for frying in a deep, heavy pan. When hot, add the dough balls and fry over a low heat until golden brown all over. Remove with a slotted spoon to drain on paper towels.

Alternatively, place the dough balls on a well-greased baking sheet and bake in a 200°C/180°C fan/400°F/gas 6 oven for 30–35 minutes, turning the dough balls as needed until the crusts are patched with golden-brown spots. Remove from the oven and brush with some of the hot melted ghee.

For the *chokha*, roast the aubergine over a gas flame until the skin is charred on all sides and the flesh is soft. Alternatively, bake at 230°C/210°C fan/450°F/gas 8 for 40 minutes.

Place the aubergine in a bowl of cold water to cool, then peel away and discard the charred skin. Place the aubergine flesh in a bowl, add the mashed potatoes and tomatoes and mash together well. Add the remaining *chokha* ingredients and mix well, then taste and adjust the seasoning, if needed.

To serve, cut the hot *litti* in half and drizzle a teaspoon of hot ghee over the top. Serve the *chokha* alongside.

CHAMPARAN MUTTON CURRY

This dish has its roots in Champaran, a district of Bihar. The meat is steam-cooked in a rich mix of mustard oil, onions and ginger with whole garlic bulbs until very tender. Traditionally made in a *handi* (earthenware pot) sealed with dough to trap the steam inside, it would have been cooked slowly over the embers of a wood fire.

Serves 4

500g/1lb 2oz boneless mutton
2 tbsp coriander seeds
1 tbsp cumin seeds
200ml/7fl oz/scant 1 cup mustard oil
3 dried red chillies
2 black cardamom pods
3–4 green cardamom pods
4–5 cloves
1 bay leaf
350g/12oz onions, chopped
3 green chillies, slit
2 whole garlic bulbs, unpeeled
1 cinnamon stick
½ tsp fennel seeds, crushed
1 tsp Kashmiri red chilli powder
200ml/7fl oz/scant 1 cup water
2 tbsp chopped coriander/cilantro
salt, to taste

DOUGH

150g/5oz/1 cup plain/all-purpose wholemeal/wholewheat flour
½ tsp salt

MARINADE

2 tsp salt
1 tsp ground turmeric
1 tsp hot chilli powder
1 tsp Garam Masala (store-bought or see page 12)
4–5 black peppercorns, crushed
1 tbsp ground coriander
2 tsp ground cumin
1 tbsp Ginger-Garlic Paste (see page 17)
100g/3½oz/generous ⅓ cup plain yogurt

First, make the dough by mixing together the flour and salt in a bowl. Gradually add water, as much as needed, to form a dough. Knead until firm and smooth. Set aside.

Cut the mutton into bite-size chunks, place in a separate bowl and add all the marinade ingredients. Mix well and set aside while you prepare the gravy.

In a frying pan, dry-roast the coriander seeds and cumin seeds, then crush them with a pestle and mortar.

Heat 150ml/5fl oz/⅔ cup of the mustard oil in a clay pot, casserole dish or a heavy pan (that has a tight-fitting lid) over a medium heat. When hot, add the dried red chillies, black and green cardamom pods, cloves and bay leaf. Once they start crackling, add the chopped onions and sauté for 5–7 minutes. Once they start turning golden brown, add the marinated mutton along with the green chillies, whole garlic bulbs, cinnamon stick, crushed coriander and cumin seeds, fennel powder and Kashmiri chilli powder.

Add the remaining mustard oil to the pot/pan along with the measured water. Roll the dough into a long sausage shape and place it around the edges of the pot/pan. Place the lid on top and press into the dough to seal. Cook over a low heat for 45 minutes, shaking the pot/pan from time to time.

Remove from the heat, remove the dough from the edges of the pot/pan and open the lid. Check that the meat is cooked and adjust the seasoning to taste. Garnish with the choppped fresh coriander and serve with chapati.

BIHARI BESAN KA SABJI

Besan ki sabji is a chickpea dumpling curry that is also cooked in Rajasthan, where it is called *gatte ki sabji*. The Rajasthani version is cooked in a yogurt base with fenugreek leaves and cylindrical dumplings, whereas the Bihari version is cooked differently, with little square dumplings in a spicy tomato-based sauce. *Pictured overleaf (left).*

Serves 4

DUMPLINGS
125g/4oz/generous 1 cup gram flour/besan
½ tsp carom seeds/ajwain
½ tsp Kashmiri chilli powder
¼ tsp ground cumin
½ tsp ground coriander
1 tsp salt
100ml/3½fl oz/scant ½ cup water, or as needed
1 tbsp rapeseed/canola oil, plus extra for deep-frying and greasing

CURRY SAUCE
1 tbsp mustard oil
1 bay leaf
1 tsp cumin seeds
100g/3½oz Fried Onion Paste (see page 17)
1 tbsp Ginger-Garlic Paste (see page 17)
½ tsp hot chilli powder
½ tsp ground cumin
1 tsp ground coriander
1½ tsp Garam Masala (store-bought or see page 12)
50g/1¾oz tomato paste/tomato concentrate
100ml/3½fl oz/scant ½ cup water
salt, to taste
2 tbsp chopped fresh coriander/cilantro, to garnish

In a large bowl, combine all the ingredients for the dumplings, except the oil, adding the water gradually and mixing well until you have a smooth pancake-like batter.

Heat the tablespoon of oil in a non-stick frying pan over a medium heat. Add the batter to the pan and cook, stirring constantly, until the batter starts to come together in a ball. Transfer the batter to a greased plate and knead with your hands until you have an almost smooth dough. Gently flatten out the dough with your fingers to a slab that is 1cm/½in thick. Use a sharp knife to cut out 5cm/2in squares of the dough.

Heat enough oil for deep-frying in a deep, heavy pan over a medium heat. When hot, deep-fry the dumpling squares, flipping until golden on both sides. Remove with a slotted spoon to drain on paper towels.

To make the curry sauce, heat the tablespoon of mustard oil until smoking, then reduce the heat to medium and add the bay leaf and cumin seeds. Once the seeds start to splutter, add the fried onion paste, ginger-garlic paste, chilli powder, ground cumin, ground coriander and garam masala, and cook until the oil starts to separate. Add the tomato paste and cook for 3–5 minutes, then add the measured water and stir well. Add salt to taste.

Add the fried chickpea dumplings to the curry and let it simmer over a low heat, uncovered, for about 5 minutes. The dumplings will absorb a considerable amount of liquid, so feel free to add some more hot water to the mix to thin out the gravy to the desired consistency. Remove from the heat, garnish with the chopped fresh coriander and let it sit covered for 5 minutes before serving.

Serve hot with rice or chapatis.

BIHARI CHICKEN CURRY

This hearty curry is a traditional dish from Bihar, where chicken pieces are marinated in a mixture of yogurt and spices, and are then slow-cooked to perfection with onions, ginger and green chillies. Chicken on the bone is the meat of choice, but if you prefer boneless chicken, you can use that too. *Pictured overleaf (right).*

Serves 4

- 500g/1lb 2oz chicken legs or thighs (on-the-bone or boneless, as you prefer)
- 100g/3½oz/generous ⅓ cup Greek-style yogurt
- 1 tsp ground turmeric
- 1 tsp Garam Masala (store-bought or see page 12)
- 1 tsp salt, or to taste
- 100ml/3½fl oz/scant ½ cup mustard oil
- 2.5cm/1in cinnamon stick
- 2 bay leaves
- 6–7 black peppercorns
- 2 black cardamom pods
- 3–4 green cardamom pods
- 4–5 cloves
- 250g/9oz onions, sliced
- 2 garlic cloves
- 2.5cm/1in piece of fresh root ginger
- 3–4 green chillies (alter the amount to suit your taste)
- 2 tsp ground coriander
- 1 tsp chilli powder
- 1 tsp Kashmiri chilli powder
- 100ml/3½fl oz/scant ½ cup water
- 2 tbsp chopped fresh coriander/cilantro leaves

Place the chicken pieces in a large bowl, add the yogurt, ground turmeric, garam masala and salt, and toss so that the chicken is well coated. Leave to marinate for 10–15 minutes.

Heat the mustard oil in a large pan over a medium-high heat until it starts to smoke slightly, then add cinnamon stick, bay leaves, peppercorns, cardamom pods and cloves. Let them sizzle for a few seconds. Add the sliced onions and a pinch of salt to the pan and sauté until the onions are golden brown. Add the whole garlic cloves and sauté for another minute.

Crush the ginger and green chillies to a paste using a pestle and mortar (or just finely chop). Add to the pan and sauté for a minute. Stir in the ground coriander and chilli powders, and sauté until the spices are fragrant. Add the marinated chicken to the pan and sauté over a medium-high heat for 2–3 minutes.

Once the masala starts to coat the chicken and become thick, add the measured water to create a flavourful gravy. Let the chicken simmer for a further 15–20 minutes until tender.

Just before serving, stir in the chopped coriander leaves and cook for a final 1–2 minutes. Serve hot with steamed rice or chapatis.

BIHARI ALOO BHUJIYA

This is a very simple, home-style potato recipe. If you love potato fries, then you must try this crunchy Bihari dish that is packed with flavour. Serve as a side dish, as a main with parathas and dal, or you can even try it for breakfast with parathas and pickle.

Serves 4

2 tbsp mustard oil
1 tsp cumin seeds
2 green chillies, chopped
1 tbsp finely chopped fresh root ginger
250g/9oz potatoes, cut lengthwise into thin fries (peeled or not – your choice)
½ tsp ground turmeric
2 tbsp chopped fresh coriander/cilantro
juice of ½ lime
salt, to taste

Heat the oil in a non-stick wok (that has a lid) over a medium heat. When hot, add the cumin seeds and let splutter, then add the green chillies and ginger, and sauté briefly. Add the potato fries and mix well, then add the ground turmeric and a pinch of salt. Reduce the heat to low, cover and cook, stirring occasionally, until the potatoes are cooked through, about 10–12 minutes. If they start sticking to the pan, sprinkle with a few drops of water.

Toward the end, when the potatoes are almost done, remove the lid and allow them to become crispy, stirring frequently so they all cook evenly. Check the seasoning, then remove from the heat, add the chopped coriander and lime juice, and mix well.

Transfer to a serving bowl and serve.

BIHARI CHANA DAL PURI

Dal puri is a popular breakfast dish of stuffed, fried breads, which you will also find served in roadside shops. It is a common dish to find served at weddings in northern India, but there it will usually be stuffed with white lentils and served with a potato and black pepper curry along with curd/yogurt. Serve hot with Mint and Coriander Chutney (see page 18) and pickles.

Serves 4

STUFFING
100g/3½oz/generous ½ cup chana dal
250ml/9fl oz/1 cup water
1 tsp salt
3 tbsp rapeseed/canola oil
1 tsp cumin seeds
1 tsp Kashmiri chilli powder
1 tsp ground coriander
¼ tsp ground turmeric
pinch of asafoetida
1 tbsp finely chopped fresh coriander/cilantro (optional)

DOUGH
200g/7oz/1⅓ cups plain/all-purpose wholemeal/wholewheat flour
25g/1oz fine semolina
1 tsp salt

250ml/9fl oz/1 cup rapeseed/canola oil, for deep-frying

Start with the stuffing. Rinse the dal in cold water, then leave it to soak in a bowl of fresh water for 10–15 minutes. Drain.

Put the measured water in a pan along with ½ teaspoon of the salt, add the drained lentils and bring to the boil. Simmer for 12–15 minutes until the dal is soft enough to mash. Keep checking on the dal and do not overcook it. Once cooked, leave to cool, then drain and mash.

Heat the oil in a wide pan over a medium heat. Add the cumin seeds and let crackle, then add the mashed chana dal, chilli powder, ground coriander, turmeric, asafoetida and remaining ½ teaspoon of salt. Mix well and cook for about 2–3 minutes, then mix in the chopped fresh coriander (if using). Remove to a bowl to cool.

For the dough, combine the flour, semolina and salt in a mixing bowl. Add enough water to bring the dough together, mixing well, then knead into a soft dough. Cover with a damp cloth and set aside for about 30 minutes.

Heat the oil for deep-frying in a wide, deep frying pan.

Divide the dough into 8–10 equal-sized balls and divide the stuffing mixture into the same number of portions. Roll out each ball of dough to a disc, 6cm/2¼in in diameter. Place a portion of stuffing in the middle of each, then carefully bring all the edges of the dough in to enclose the stuffing well. Gently flatten out into small circles, about 8cm/3in in diameter, making sure the stuffing does not come out.

One at a time, carefully transfer each puri to the hot oil and fry until puffed and golden brown on each side, flipping halfway through. Remove with a slotted spoon to drain on paper towels. Repeat until all the puris are cooked.

Serve hot with chutney and pickles.

MAKHANA KHEER

This sweet pudding is a key part of the Indian festival of Navratri and is particularly popular as it can be eaten during fasting periods. Lotus seeds, or fox nuts, are a common snack food in Indian households. Gluten-free and protein-rich, they can be eaten as a kind of popcorn or made into this delicious dessert. This is so easy to make and it can be served both chilled and hot. I particularly like to eat it hot during the winter season.

Serves 4

2 tbsp ghee
100g/3½oz puffed lotus seeds (phool makhana/fox nuts)
1 litre/35fl oz/4¼ cups whole milk
½ tsp saffron strands
¼ tsp ground cardamom
50g/1¾oz/¼ cup jaggery powder
10–15 pistachio slivers, to decorate

Heat the ghee in a non-stick frying pan, add the lotus seeds and sauté over a medium heat for 3–4 minutes, or until crispy. Do not let them burn. Remove from the heat and leave to cool.

When cool, either break the lotus seeds into smaller pieces or place in a food processor and blitz to a coarse powder, as you wish. Some people prefer more texture in the finished dessert, while others like it smoother. Set aside.

In a large pan, boil the milk until it starts to thicken, then add the lotus seeds/powder and cook for a few minutes. Add the saffron and ground cardamom, then when the *kheer* has thickened to your liking, remove from the heat and stir in the jaggery powder.

Unless serving hot, refrigerate the *makhana kheer* for at least 1 hour and serve chilled, decorated with the pistachio slivers.

LAUNG LATA

This famous Bihari sweet has many names – you might also see it referred to as *lavang lata* or *latika*. These crispy pastry parcels are filled with a sweet mixture of *mawa/khoya* (a dried milk product) and nuts, and are sealed with a clove (*lavang*), which lends an exotic aroma. Served warm, they are rich and delicious. I always advise to buy *mawa/khoya* ready-made, at Indian grocery stores or online, as it is very time-consuming to make from scratch.

Makes about 10–12

200g/7oz/generous 1½ cups plain/all-purpose flour
2 tbsp fine semolina
¼ tsp baking powder
⅛ tsp salt
2 tbsp ghee or cooking oil, plus extra for deep-frying
10–12 cloves
crushed pistachios, to decorate

FILLING

1 tbsp ghee or cooking oil
50g/1¾oz mixed nuts (almonds, cashews and pistachios), finely chopped
150g/5oz *mawa/khoya* (dried milk product – buy ready-made at Indian grocery stores or online)
2 tbsp granulated sugar
2–3 drops kewra water (or rose water)
⅛ tsp freshly crushed green cardamom seeds

SUGAR SYRUP

400g/14oz/generous 1¾ cups granulated sugar
400ml/14fl oz/1⅔ cups water
1–2 drops lemon juice
a few saffron strands
3–4 drops rose water

Put the flour, semolina, baking powder and salt on a large plate and add the ghee or oil to it. Mix well with your hands. Add just enough water to form a medium-stiff dough. The dough should neither be very soft nor very stiff. Set aside.

For the filling, heat the ghee or oil in a heavy pan over a low heat. Add the nuts and sauté for a couple of minutes, then add the *mawa/khoya* and sauté until it turns lightly golden. Transfer the mixture to a plate, add the sugar to it and mix well. Leave to cool, then add the kewra water and crushed cardamom seeds to the mixture and mix well.

Divide the dough into 10–12 small balls of equal size and roll them into thin oval shapes, about 8 x 4cm/3 x 1½in. Place some filling mixture in the centre of each oval and fold in the 2 long edges to enclose. Now fold over the 2 short sides (rather like sealing an envelope) and close the fold with a clove to hold it in place. Continue to form the pastries until all the dough and filling has been used up.

Make the sugar syrup. In a saucepan, combine the sugar and measured water, and heat over a high heat, stirring until the sugar has dissolved. Add the lemon juice, saffron and rose water, and continue to stir for about 5 minutes until the syrup is thick and sticky. Reduce the heat to very low.

Meanwhile, heat enough ghee or oil for deep-frying in a deep, heavy pan over a high heat. When hot, reduce the heat and start frying the pastries, one by one, until light golden on each side.

Remove the cooked *laung lata* from the oil with a slotted spoon and place them in the sugar syrup. Turn until well coated, then remove to a plate. Do not leave the *laung lata* in the syrup or they will become soft. Decorate with crushed pistachios and serve either hot or at room temperature.

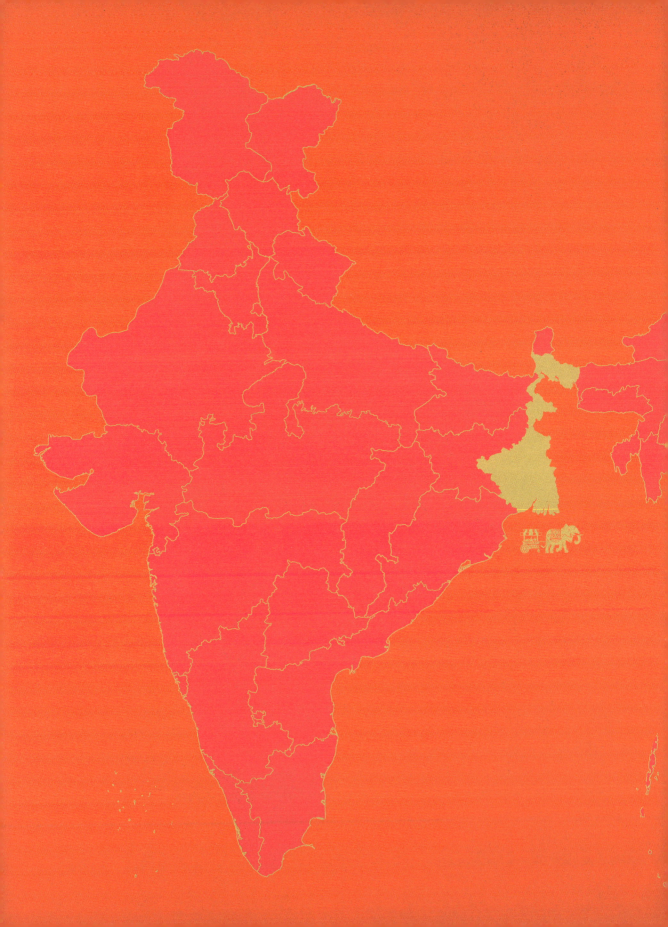

WEST BENGAL

WEST BENGAL

West Bengal is located in eastern India and its cuisine has been shaped by the region's diverse history. Encompassing influences from Bangladesh, which it borders on the east, the region had strong historical links with Britain, Western Asia and the rest of the world due to its status as a trade hub and epicentre of the British Raj. Influences from all over the world entered its culinary repertoire as a result. Its unique history with Hindu widows also came to bear on the cuisine. The historical repression of widowed women in the region, which famously ended in 1856 with the Re-marriage Act, extended as far as dictating their diets: "heating" or "bitter" foods such as garlic and onion were forbidden, as were meat and fish, and some of the more extravagant spices, but ginger was allowed. Hence arose a diverse vegetarian cuisine that makes delicious use of the cheaper spices and heavily leans on ginger.

Staples of the region are rice, fish, lentils and vegetables, with *maach* (fish) and *bhaat* (rice) being an essential in almost every household. Mustard oil is used widely, as are white poppy seeds. Bengali food has a reputation for being extremely well-balanced and varied in its flavours. Careful attention is given to the six Ayurvedic principles: hot, sour, salty, sweet, bitter and *kosha* (which roughly translates as umami). Famous dishes include the aromatic fish curry, *Macher Jhol* (see page 98); the cardamom-spiced, yogurt-based curry, *Rezala* (see my chicken version on page 96); potatoes with poppy seeds, *Aloo Posto* (page 99); and the beautiful cheesecake-like steamed yogurt dessert, *Bhapa Doi* (page 108).

BEGUN BHAJA

This is a traditional Bengali-style dish of delicately spiced aubergine/eggplant fritters, fried to a crisp and usually served with a simple, homely meal. The recipe requires little time and effort, and makes an ideal appetizer to serve with drinks, or can be served as a starter or side dish.

Serves 6–8

1 tsp Kashmiri chilli powder
1 tsp ground turmeric
1 tsp dried mango powder/amchur
1 tsp Bengali Garam Masala (store-bought or see page 13)
1 tsp Ginger-Garlic Paste (see page 17)
pinch of salt, or to taste
2 tbsp lemon juice
1 large aubergine/eggplant, sliced into 1cm/½in roundels
250ml/9fl oz/1 cup mustard oil, for shallow-frying

In a bowl, combine the chilli powder, turmeric, dried mango powder, garam masala, ginger-garlic paste, salt and lemon juice. Mix well.

Lay the aubergine slices out on a plate and sprinkle the prepared spice paste over them. Rub the paste into the aubergine slices with your fingers so they are all evenly coated.

Heat the mustard oil in a large frying pan over a medium-high heat until smoking hot. As soon as the oil begins to smoke, reduce the heat to very low and arrange the aubergine slices in the pan in a single layer (you may need to cook them in batches). Pan-fry for 3–4 minutes on each side until golden, then remove with a slotted spoon to drain on paper towels.

Serve immediately, either on its own as a starter, or with dal and rice for a comforting meal.

MANGSHER JHOL

This Bengali mutton curry is ideal for a comforting, substantial weekend meal. With generous spicing, a deep red gravy and plump, golden potatoes, it makes an attractive, flavourful dish that goes well with a side of simple steamed rice.

Serves 4

800g/1lb 12oz mutton, cut into bite-size chunks (if possible, ask your butcher to add in a few extra chunks of liver and mutton fat too), washed and patted dry
5 tbsp mustard oil
100g/3½oz/generous ⅓ cup plain Greek-style yogurt
1 tbsp Kashmiri chilli powder
1 tbsp ground coriander
1 tbsp Bengali Garam Masala (store-bought or see page 13)
1 tsp ground turmeric, plus an extra pinch for the potatoes
1½ tsp granulated sugar
1 tsp salt, or to taste
150g/5oz potatoes, peeled and cut in to 2.5cm/1in chunks
3 bay leaves
4 dried red chillies
2.5cm/1in cinnamon stick
6 green cardamom pods
250g/9oz onions, finely chopped
2 tbsp Ginger-Garlic Paste (see page 17)
6 green chillies, thinly sliced
750ml/26fl oz/3¼ cups freshly boiled water
1 tsp ghee

Place the mutton chunks (and liver and fat pieces too, if you have them) in a large bowl and add 2 tablespoons of the mustard oil along with the yogurt, chilli powder, ground coriander, ½ tablespoon of the garam masala, the turmeric, sugar and salt. Mix well and leave to marinate for 20–30 minutes.

Meanwhile, place the potato chunks in a bowl, sprinkle with a little salt and ground turmeric, and toss to coat.

Heat the remaining 3 tablespoons of oil in a deep pan until hot, add the potatoes and fry until golden and cooked through. Remove with a slotted spoon to a plate and set aside.

To the same oil, add the bay leaves, dried red chillies, cinnamon stick and cardamom pods and let sizzle briefly, then add the chopped onions and fry until translucent. Add the ginger-garlic paste and sliced green chillies, and cook until the raw aromas are gone. Add the marinated mutton chunks along with the marinade to the pan and mix well. Keep the heat low and cook for around 7–8 minutes.

Place the fried potatoes on top of the meat and start adding the boiling water to the pan, just until the water covers both meat and potatoes. Cover and cook over a low heat until the meat is tender.

Add the remaining ½ tablespoon of garam masala and the ghee, give the curry a final mix, then check the seasoning. Serve hot with steamed rice.

MURGI JHOL

This Bengali home-style chicken and potato curry, flavoured with aromatic whole spices, is spicy, delicious and soupy. It makes a quick and easy Sunday supper, best eaten with piping hot rice with a squeeze of lime.

Serves 4

100g/3½oz onion, chopped
2 tbsp finely chopped fresh root ginger
6–7 large garlic cloves, chopped
3 tbsp plain yogurt
750g/1lb 10oz on-the-bone chicken pieces
1 tsp Kashmiri chilli powder
1 tsp chilli powder
½ tsp ground turmeric
1 tsp ground cumin
½ tsp ground coriander
1 tsp salt
2 tsp lime juice
1 tsp mustard oil

CURRY SAUCE

3½ tbsp mustard oil or vegetable oil
2 medium potatoes, peeled and halved
2–3 bay leaves
5cm/2in cinnamon stick, broken in half
5–6 cloves
5–6 green cardamom pods
1 tsp granulated sugar
250g/9oz onions, thinly sliced
2–3 green chillies, slit
300ml/10½fl oz/1¼ cups hot water, or as needed
½ tsp Bengali Garam Masala (see page 13)
1 tsp ghee
salt, to taste
2 tbsp chopped coriander/cilantro leaves, to garnish

Combine the onion, ginger, garlic and yogurt in a food processor and blitz to a paste.

Place the chicken in a large bowl and add the yogurt paste along with the dried spices, salt, lime juice and mustard oil. Mix with your hands until the chicken is well coated, cover and set aside for at least 30 minutes.

For the curry sauce, heat 2 tablespoons of the oil in a large, heavy pan (that has a lid) over a high heat. When hot, toss in the potatoes along with a pinch of salt and fry until golden brown. Remove with a slotted spoon and set aside.

Add the rest of the oil to the same pan and heat over a medium heat. Add the bay leaves, cinnamon sticks, cloves and cardamom pods. Once they start to crackle, add the sugar and let it slightly caramelize a bit, then add the sliced onions and sauté until soft and golden brown in colour.

Add the marinated chicken along with its marinade and cook, stirring continuously, for 9–10 minutes.

Add the fried potatoes to the curry along with another pinch of salt and mix well. Cover and cook for a further 10 minutes.

When the mixture looks dry, add the green chillies and hot water (adjust the amount of water to your liking, adding more if you prefer a thinner sauce) and bring to the boil.

Cover and cook over a medium heat until the chicken and the potatoes are cooked through. Check the seasoning and add more salt or sugar, if required.

Add the Bengali garam masala and ghee, mix well and cook for a final 2 minutes. Remove from the heat, sprinkle with the fresh coriander and serve hot with rice or roti or paratha.

CHICKEN REZALA

Bengali chicken *rezala* is a creamy curry with a thin yogurt gravy that brings all the flavours and personality of the north-eastern region of India to the fore. Mustard oil and white poppy seeds play a central role in creating a dish brimming with flavour and a rich, luxurious texture.

Serves 4

- 800g/1lb 12oz skinless chicken (on-the-bone or boneless), cut into 5cm/2in chunks
- 1 tbsp Ginger-Garlic Paste (see page 17)
- 100g/3½oz/generous ⅓ cup plain yogurt
- 4 tbsp white poppy seeds
- 3 tbsp warm water
- 4–5 green chillies
- 2 tbsp mustard oil
- 4 tbsp ghee
- 3–4 cloves
- 6–8 black peppercorns
- 5cm/2in cinnamon stick
- 2 green cardamom pods
- 2 black cardamom pods
- 4–5 whole dried red chillies
- 250g/9oz Fried Onion Paste (see page 17)
- 1 tsp white pepper
- 2 tsp salt
- 1 tsp Bengali Garam Masala (store-bought or see page 13)
- 2–3 drops kewra essence
- pinch of saffron strands soaked in 1 tbsp milk
- a few fresh coriander/cilantro leaves, to garnish

Combine the chicken, ginger-garlic paste and yogurt in a bowl, cover and leave to marinate in the refrigerator for 1 hour.

Soak the poppy seeds in the measured warm water for 10 minutes.

Transfer the poppy seeds with their soaking water to a food processor along with the green chillies and blitz to a smooth paste.

Heat the mustard oil along with 3 tablespoons of the ghee in a large pan (that has a tight-fitting lid) over a medium-high heat. When hot, add the cloves, peppercorns, cinnamon stick, cardamom pods and dried red chillies to the pan and sauté for 10–15 seconds. Add the onion paste, reduce the heat to low and cook until the raw aroma goes away. Add the marinated chicken and mix well. Add the poppy-seed paste, white pepper, salt and garam masala and mix well. Cover and cook for 35 minutes until the chicken is thoroughly cooked, stirring from time to time.

Add the remaining tablespoon of ghee along with the kewra essence and mix well. Check the seasoning, then garnish with the saffron soaked in milk and serve sprinkled with a few coriander leaves, with rice and maybe some mango chutney.

MACHER JHOL

This renowned Bengali-style curry consists of chunks or slices of fish slowly simmered in a flavourful broth that is usually enriched with onions, ginger and spices. Many people also add chunks of potato and aubergine/eggplant to cook along with the fish. *Macher jhol* is usually served with rice. *Pictured overleaf (left).*

Serves 4–5

4 white fish fillets (cod or sea bass, for example)
2 tbsp ground turmeric
6 tbsp mustard oil
1–2 large potatoes, cut into 12–16 wedges
8–10 baby aubergines/eggplants
1 tsp nigella seeds
2 tsp cumin seeds
1 tsp fenugreek seeds
400g/14oz onions, finely chopped
4 tsp ginger paste
2 tsp garlic paste
2 tsp red chilli powder
2 tbsp ground cumin
2 tsp ground coriander
870ml/30fl oz/3¾ cups water
300g/10½oz fresh or canned tomatoes, finely chopped
4–6 green chillies, slit (reduce to taste, or leave out if you don't like too much heat)
2 tsp lemon juice
4 tbsp chopped fresh coriander/cilantro leaves
salt, to taste

Sprinkle the fish fillets with the turmeric and a pinch of salt each, then set aside for 10–15 minutes.

Heat the mustard oil in a large pan over a high heat. When hot, sear the fish fillets for about 2 minutes on each side. Remove with a slotted spoon to a plate and set aside. Add the potato wedges and fry until golden on all sides, then remove and set aside. Add the baby aubergines and fry until soft, then remove and set aside.

To the same pan, add the nigella, cumin and fenugreek seeds. Once they start to crackle, add the chopped onions and sauté over a medium heat until golden brown. Add the ginger and garlic pastes, and cook for couple of minutes until the raw smells goes away.

Mix the ground spices into 120ml/4fl oz/½ cup of the water, then add to the pan along with another pinch of salt. Mix well and cook for 2–3 minutes. Add the tomatoes and cook over a low heat until the tomatoes turn mushy. Add the fried fish, potatoes, aubergines and green chillies to the pan along with the remaining 750ml/26fl oz/3¼ cups water and bring to a rolling boil. Cook for 3–4 minutes, then remove from the heat and stir in the lemon juice.

Serve garnished with the fresh coriander.

ALOO POSTO

This is a traditional Bengali recipe of potatoes cooked in a poppy-seed paste, that you can easily prepare and serve at home along with *Luchhi* (see page 106). Ideally enjoyed for breakfast, aloo posto can also be enjoyed as a side to other dishes such as dal. This is a light dish with a subtle spiciness to it. *Pictured overleaf (right).*

Serves 4

10 tbsp poppy seeds
splash of water or coconut milk
4 tbsp vegetable oil
1 tsp nigella seeds
1 tsp cumin seeds
8 large potatoes, par-boiled and diced
8 medium green chillies, finely chopped
1 tsp salt
1 tsp ground turmeric
juice of 1 lime
4 tbsp chopped fresh coriander/cilantro

Place the poppy seeds in a blender along with the splash of water or coconut milk and blitz to a paste. Set aside.

Heat the oil in a wide pan over a medium heat. When hot, add the nigella and cumin seeds. Once they start to crackle, add the potatoes and fry them well until golden brown in colour.

Add the poppy-seed paste along with the fresh green chillies. Stir once, then add the salt and turmeric. Stir well and cook for 2 minutes. If the dish is too dry, add a splash of water and stir again.

Remove from the heat and add the lime juice and fresh coriander. Serve with *luchhi*.

CHINGRI MALAI KARI

This iconic Bengali curry of black tiger prawns/shrimp or freshwater prawns cooked in a subtle, creamy coconut-milk sauce is very quick and easy to make. It's versatile too – you can swap out the prawns for white fish, if you prefer.

Serves 4

- 20–24 tiger or freshwater prawns/shrimp, shelled and deveined with the tails left on
- 1 tsp ground turmeric
- 200g/7oz onions, roughly chopped
- 100ml/3½fl oz/scant ½ cup mustard oil
- 2 tbsp ghee
- 2–3 dried red chillies
- 1 bay leaf
- 4 green cardamom pods
- 4–6 cloves
- 6cm/2¼in cinnamon stick
- 1 tbsp sugar
- 20g/¾oz/4 tsp ginger paste
- 1 tsp Kashmiri chilli powder
- 6 green chillies, slit
- 300ml/10½fl oz/1¼ cups coconut milk
- 75g/2½oz/generous ¼ cup plain yogurt
- ½ tsp Bengali Garam Masala (store-bought or see page 13)
- handful of chopped fresh coriander/cilantro
- salt, to taste

Place the prawns in a bowl along with ½ teaspoon salt and ½ teaspoon of the turmeric. Set aside to marinate.

Place the onions in a food processor along with a splash of water and blitz to a fine paste. Set aside.

Heat the mustard oil in a large pan over a medium heat. Add the marinated prawns and sauté briefly for just 1–2 minutes. Remove from the pan with a slotted spoon and set aside.

Add the ghee to the the same pan, then add the dried red chillies, bay leaf, cardamom, cloves and cinnamon, and sauté briefly. Add the onion paste along with the sugar and fry for about 10–15 minutes until the onion paste turns brown.

Add the ginger paste and fry for another 3–4 minutes until the raw aroma goes away, then add the remaining ½ teaspoon of turmeric along with the Kashmiri chilli powder, green chillies and ½ teaspoon salt. Cook, stirring occasionally, so that the onion and spices don't stick to the bottom of the pan – if they do, add a splash of the coconut milk. Once the oil starts separating from the spices, remove the pan from the heat and stir in the yogurt, stirring vigorously to prevent the yogurt from splitting. Put the pan back on the heat and cook for 3–4 minutes. Add the coconut milk and simmer for about 5 minutes. Add the prawns and simmer for a final 5 minutes.

Sprinkle with the garam masala and chopped coriander, then serve.

MASOOR DAL

Bengali *masoor dal* is a simple but delicious lentil dish that will complement any Indian meal. During the summer season, Bengalis like to eat lentils almost every day, along with plain rice, because they are easy to digest.

Serves 4

- 200g/7oz/generous 1 cup masoor dal/split red lentils, rinsed, soaked and drained
- ½ tsp ground turmeric
- 650ml/22fl oz/2¾ cups water
- 3 tbsp mustard oil
- ½ tsp brown mustard seeds
- 1 tsp Panch Phoran (store-bought or see page 14)
- 125g/4oz onions, chopped
- 2 green chillies, chopped
- 2 tbsp Ginger-Garlic Paste (see page 17)
- 1 tsp Kashmiri chilli powder
- 1 tsp salt, or to taste
- 75g/2½oz tomatoes, chopped
- 1 tbsp chopped fresh coriander/cilantro
- juice of ½ lime

In a large pan (that has a lid), combine the drained soaked lentils and turmeric with the measured water. Bring to the boil, uncovered, then reduce the heat to low, cover and simmer for 20–25 minutes until the lentils are soft.

Meanwhile, heat the mustard oil in a frying pan over a medium heat. Add the mustard seeds and panch phoran. When they start to crackle, add the chopped onions and green chillies, reduce the heat to low and cook until the onions soften and turn light brown. Increase the heat to medium, stir in the ginger-garlic paste and cook for about 2–3 minutes. Add the chilli powder and salt, stir well and cook for another minute or so. Add the tomatoes and cook, stirring frequently, until the tomatoes soften. You know you are done when the skins starts to come away from the tomato flesh.

Fold the tomato mixture into the lentils, then taste and adjust the salt. Sprinkle with the coriander and lime juice. Serve hot.

LUCHHI

Luchhi are deep-fried flatbreads that are especially popular in West Bengal. They are similar to *poori*, which are made with wholemeal/wholewheat flour. Getting them to puff up well during frying takes a little practice, but they will still be soft and delicious either way. Serve with your curry of choice.

Serves 4

240g/8½oz/scant 2 cups plain/all-purpose flour, plus extra if needed
2½ tbsp ghee
½ tsp salt
150ml/5fl oz/⅔ cup water, or as needed
300ml/10½fl oz/1¼ cups rapeseed/canola oil, plus extra for brushing

In a large bowl, combine the flour, ghee and salt, mixing well. Add 3 tablespoons of the water and mix well with your hands or with a spatula. Slowly add the remaining water, as needed, kneading well until you have a very soft and smooth dough. If you find the dough becomes sticky, add some extra flour and knead in well. Cover the dough with a damp cloth and leave to rest at room temperature for at least 30 minutes.

Heat the 300ml/10½fl oz/1¼ cups rapeseed/canola oil in a kadai or large pan until hot enough for deep-frying, about 180°C/350°F. To test it, drop a small piece of the dough into the oil – if it pops up quickly from the bottom, it means the oil is ready for the *luchhi* to be fried.

Divide the rested dough into 6–8 balls of equal size. While you are working, keep the balls covered with a damp cloth. Apply a little oil to one of the balls and use a rolling pin to roll it out to a 13cm/5in disc.

Gently lower the bread carefully into the hot oil. The *luchhi* will begin to puff up. Gently nudge it with a spoon to help it puff up well. When one side has become lightly golden in colour and the oil has stopped sizzling, turn it over and fry the other side. Don't allow it to become too crispy. Remove to drain on paper towels.

Roll out and fry the remaining *luchhi* in the same way – working in batches is best.

Serve hot.

ROSE SANDESH

This are some of the most famous Bengali sweets, which are so easy to make at home. Lots of people make them with ready-made paneer (cottage cheese), but I prefer to make fresh cheese from scratch. This method will give you a very soft textured, quality *sandesh*. There are plain versions, but I flavour it with rose water and dried rose petals for a lovely twist.

Serves 4

850ml/30fl oz/generous 3½ cups whole/full-fat milk
5 tbsp lemon juice
1 tbsp ground almonds
1 tbsp dried rose petals
3 tbsp icing/confectioners' sugar, or to taste
½ tsp rose water
¼ tsp ground cardamom
2 tbsp chopped nuts of choice (such as almonds or pistachios), to decorate

Bring the milk to the boil in a heavy pan over a medium heat, stirring continuously. Add the lemon juice and stir well. When you see the milk begin to curdle, turn off the heat. Make sure it is well curdled and allow to settle for a minute.

Place a colander in the sink and line it with a muslin cloth/cheesecloth. Pour in the curdled milk to drain off the whey. Slowly rinse the curds under cold running water (this will help reduce the lemon taste). Squeeze out any excess water, make a knot in the cloth and leave it to hang (perhaps over the tap or over a cupboard handle with a bowl placed underneath) for an hour or so to drain further.

The resulting fresh cheese is paneer. Add the paneer to a plate or mixing bowl and knead it well by hand. Once the mixture becomes smooth, add the ground almonds and dried rose petals, and mix well.

Heat a non-stick or heavy pan over a very low heat. Transfer the mixture to the pan and add the icing sugar, rose water and ground cardamom. Mix well, then taste for sweetness and adjust the sugar to suit. Cook for about 4–5 minutes, stirring constantly so that it doesn't stick to the pan. Overcooking will make the mixture grainy, so take care not to cook it for too long. Remove from the heat and leave to cool completely.

When cool, turn out the mixture onto the work surface and knead lightly. Divide the mixture into small balls, rolling with both hands until smooth. Place on a plate, flatten each ball a little, then decorate the top of each sweet with chopped nuts. Refrigerate for an hour or so before serving.

BHAPA DOI

This is one of my all-time favourite Indian desserts. A dish of steamed yogurt with a texture similar to cheesecake, it is very easy to make. I like to flavour it with rose and serve with seasonal fresh berries and a sweet-sour berry chutney.

Serves 6–8

250g/9oz/1 cup Greek yogurt
250ml/9fl oz/1 cup condensed milk
3 tbsp double/heavy cream
1 tsp rose water
2 tbsp dried rose petals
50g/1¾oz dried cranberries
fresh mixed berries, to serve

BERRY CHUTNEY

250g/9oz fresh or frozen mixed berries
100g/3½oz/½ cup granulated sugar
2 star anise

First, make the berry chutney. Combine all the ingredients in a saucepan and stir over a medium heat until the berries completely collapse. Remove the star anise and transfer to a food processor. Blitz to a smooth paste. Transfer back to the pan and simmer, uncovered, for 10 minutes. Cool, transfer to a sterilized jar and store in the refrigerator until needed.

Combine the yogurt, condensed milk, cream, rose water and dried rose petals in a mixing bowl and mix until smooth and creamy. Refrigerate for at least 3–4 hours, or overnight.

Preheat the oven to 180°C/160°C fan/350°F/Gas 4.

Strain the yogurt mixture through a fine sieve, then add the dried cranberries and stir to combine. Pour the mixture among 6–8 small ramekins, no more than 5cm/2in in diameter. Alternatively, you can use silicone muffin moulds.

Place the filled ramekins/moulds into a deep baking tin and pour enough water around the bases to come about halfway up the sides. Bake in the oven for 20–25 minutes until an inserted toothpick comes out clean. Set aside to cool.

Once the ramekins are completely cool, chill them in the refrigerator for at least 2 hours. If using the silicone moulds, place in the freezer for 10–15 minutes, which will make it easier to unmould them.

To serve, turn the chilled *bhapa doi* out onto serving plates and decorate with fresh berries and the berry chutney.

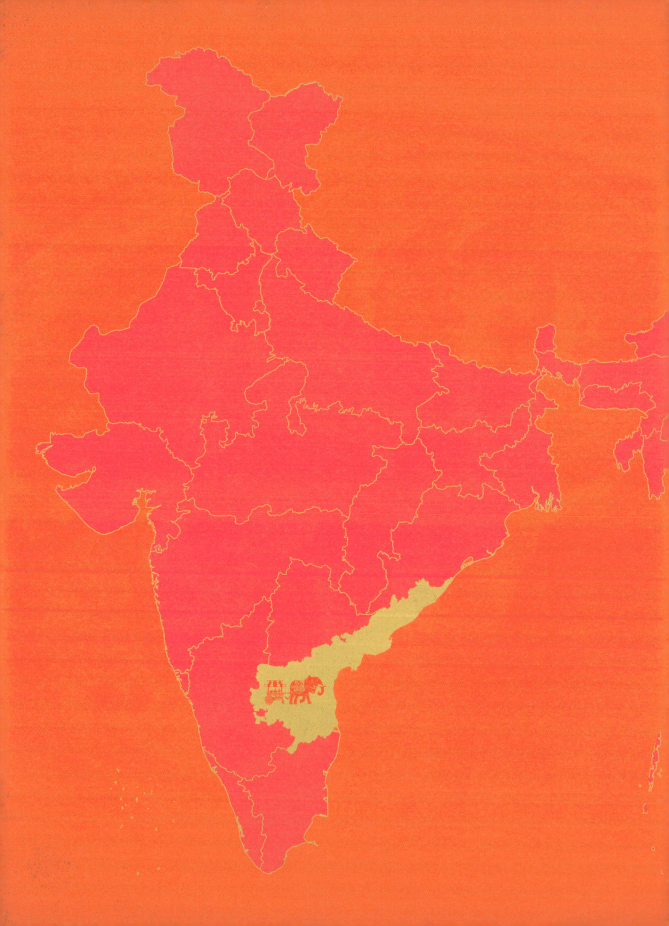

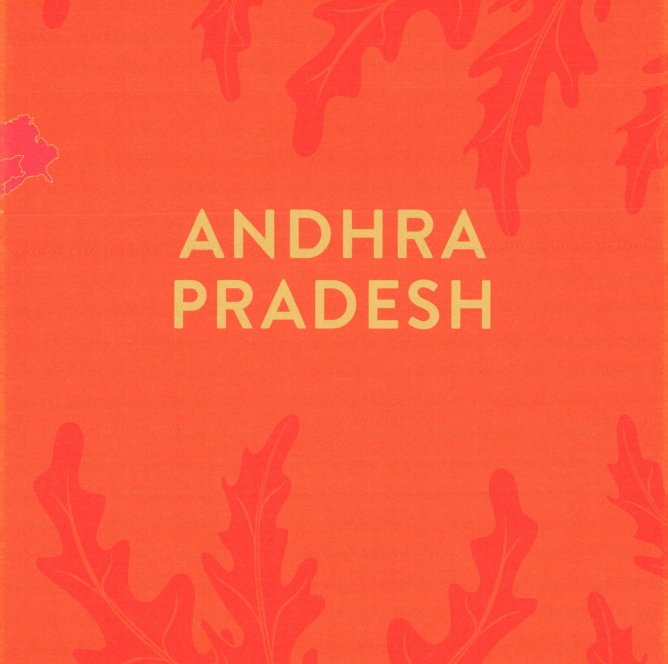

ANDHRA PRADESH

ANDHRA PRADESH

Andhra Pradesh is a state in the southern coastal region of India. Its cuisine, culturally known as Telugu cuisine, is generally known for tangy, hot and spicy flavours. This is not surprising, since Andhra Pradesh is the leading producer of red chillies in India.

Vegetarian dishes feature prominently, as well as seafood in the coastal areas, and spicy, hot varieties of pickles and chutneys are common. Tangy tamarind is another ingredient that is frequently used. You will find many opulent dishes among the region's favourites, chiefly influenced by the eating habits of the Nawabs (Hindu royals) and Brahmins, which found their way into kitchens across the state. Different communities have developed their own variations, and rural areas still follow centuries-old cooking methods and recipes.

I have chosen to feature a popular breakfast dish, *Pesarattu* (see page 114), which is a delicious *dosa*-like pancake stuffed with spiced potatoes and cheese, along with a classic Andhra Chicken Fry (page 116) and Lamb Masala (page 123). I have also included a number of recipes from the neighbouring area of Hyderabad in this chapter, as many of their dishes are common in Andhra Pradesh and are not to be missed. Notable are Hyderabadi Vegetable *Dum Biryani* (page 120) and the aubergine/eggplant dish, *Baghare Baingan* (page 117). For dessert, you must try *Double Ka Meetha* – a mouthwatering bread and butter pudding flavoured with saffron and cardamom (page 128).

ANDHRA PRADESH

PESARATTU

Pesarattu are thin, savoury pancakes, similar to *dosa*, but requiring no fermentation. They are very easy and quick to make, and are nutritious as well as tasty. These lentil crêpes are a classic Andhra breakfast staple. I have given them a nutritious stuffing of spiced potatoes and cheese. Don't just save them for mornings – they are terrific to enjoy for any meal!

Serves 4–6

200g/7oz/1 cup green moong dal/mung beans, rinsed well and drained
2 tbsp uncooked rice (any type), rinsed well and drained
2 green chillies
1 tbsp chopped fresh root ginger
1 tsp cumin seeds
¼ tsp salt
2 tbsp vegetable oil or ghee, plus extra as needed

POTATO STUFFING

250g/9oz potatoes, peeled and cubed
1 tbsp rapeseed/canola oil
½ tsp mustard seeds
50g/1¾oz onions, thinly sliced
8–10 curry leaves
1 tbsp chopped green chillies
pinch of asafoetida
1 tsp chopped fresh root ginger
¼ tsp ground turmeric
½ tsp salt, or to taste
2–3 tbsp water
2 tbsp finely chopped fresh coriander/cilantro leaves
50g/1¾oz mozzarella cheese, grated

Start with the stuffing. Boil or steam the potatoes until just cooked, then drain and set aside.

Heat the oil in a pan over a medium-low heat. Add the mustard seeds. Once they start to crackle, add the onions, curry leaves and chillies. Fry until the onions turn lightly golden. Add the asafoetida and ginger, and fry until the raw aroma of ginger goes away. Crumble the potatoes or smash them with fork and add them to the pan. Add turmeric, salt and water, and sauté for 2–3 minutes. Stir through the fresh coriander, then taste and add more salt if needed. Set aside.

Place the rinsed moong dal and rice in a large bowl, cover with fresh water and leave to soak for 4–6 hours.

Drain the dal and rice, rinse well, then drain again and transfer to a food processor. Add the green chillies, ginger, cumin seeds and salt along with just enough water to make a thick batter. Blitz to a coarse or smooth batter as you prefer. *Pesarattu* batter must be of pouring consistency, yet needs to remain reasonably thick and spreadable. If needed, add extra water to bring it to the right consistency, but do not make the batter too runny, as the *pesarattu* will not become crispy.

Using a spatula, spread a little oil or ghee over a griddle or frying pan set over a medium-low heat. Using a ladle, pour a spoonful of the batter onto the hot pan and spread the batter into a round shape. Drizzle some extra oil or ghee on the sides and in the middle of the *pesarattu* and cook for 2 minutes, then flip and cook on the other side until crisp and browned. Place a few tablespoons of the potato stuffing mixture in the centre and spread it with a spatula, then sprinkle with a little grated mozzarella and fold the *pesarattu* over.

Serve hot with Coconut Chutney (page 18) or Tomato Chutney (page 19).

ANDHRA CHICKEN FRY

This is one of my favourites – a peppery chicken fry dish, which I have served in various ways at my restaurants. This South Indian version is very easy to prepare and makes a great snack or appetizer. Serve with paratha or on its own with drinks.

Serves 4

500g/1lb 2oz boneless chicken thighs, cut into bite-size pieces
2 tbsp Ginger-Garlic Paste (see page 17)
8–10 curry leaves, finely chopped
1 tbsp chopped green chillies
1 tbsp chopped fresh coriander/cilantro, plus extra to garnish
½ tsp ground black pepper
1 tsp salt
2 tbsp lime juice
250ml/9fl oz/1 cup neutral oil
60g/2oz/½ cup cornflour/cornstarch
40g/1½oz/¼ cup rice flour
10–12 cherry tomatoes, halved
2 tbsp grated fresh coconut

ANDHRA SPICE MIX

2 tbsp coriander seeds
1 tsp cumin seeds
½ tsp fennel seeds
5cm/2in cinnamon stick
6 cloves
4 green cardamom pods
pinch of black stone flower (optional)

MASALA

3 tbsp rapeseed/canola oil
1 tsp mustard seeds
½ tsp cumin seeds
8–10 curry leaves
250g/9oz onions, finely chopped
2 tbsp chopped fresh root ginger
1 tbsp chopped garlic
1 tbsp green peppercorns
½ tsp ground turmeric
½ tsp salt, or to taste

First, make the Andhra spice mix. In a non-reactive pan, dry-roast all of the spices over a medium heat until aromatic. Leave to cool, then grind to a fine powder in a spice grinder.

Place the chicken pieces in a bowl and add the ginger-garlic paste, chopped curry leaves, green chillies, coriander, black pepper, salt and lime juice. Mix well, cover and leave to marinate in the refrigerator for 20–30 minutes.

Meanwhile, make the masala. Heat the oil in a pan over a medium heat. Add the mustard seeds, cumin seeds and curry leaves, and stir. When they start to crackle, add the onions and sauté until light golden brown, about 8–10 minutes. Add the ginger, garlic and green peppercorns and sauté for 5–6 minutes, or until the raw smells of ginger and garlic go away. Add half of the Andhra spice mix along with the turmeric and salt, and mix well. Check the seasoning, then remove from the heat and set aside.

Heat the oil in a wok or deep pan over a medium heat until shimmering.

Remove the marinated chicken from the refrigerator and give it a quick mix. Add the cornflour and rice flour and mix well. If it's too dry, sprinkle in some water to ensure everything is well coated.

When the oil is hot, fry the chicken pieces in batches until golden and crispy. Remove with a slotted spoon to drain on paper towels.

Reheat the masala over a medium heat and add the cherry tomatoes and fried chicken. Mix well, then check the seasoning.

Serve garnished with chopped coriander and grated coconut.

BAGHARE BAINGAN

This sumptuous aubergine/eggplant curry is the natural first choice of vegetarians in this region. A traditional Hyderabadi dish, it is usually served with *Hyderabadi Biryani* (see page 120), but it can be served with any kind of rice or chapatis. *Pictured overleaf.*

Serves 4

500g/1lb 2oz baby aubergines/eggplants
1 tsp salt, or to taste
3–4 tbsp rapeseed/canola oil
½ tsp cumin seeds
¼ tsp mustard seeds
¼ tsp onion seeds
150g/5oz onions, chopped
10–15 curry leaves
1 tbsp Ginger-Garlic Paste (see page 17)
120ml/4fl oz/½ cup water
½ tsp Kashmiri chilli powder
½ tsp Garam Masala (store-bought or see page 12)
1 tsp ground coriander
¼ tsp ground turmeric
3 tbsp tamarind paste
pinch of asafoetida
2 tbsp finely chopped fresh coriander/cilantro leaves

PEANUT-COCONUT PASTE

4 tbsp peanuts
2 tbsp sesame seeds
3 tbsp desiccated/dried shredded or freshly grated coconut

First, make the peanut-coconut paste. In a dry frying pan over a medium heat, dry-roast the peanuts until they begin to smell aromatic and turn golden. Reduce the heat and add the sesame seeds. When they begin to splutter, turn off the heat, add the desiccated coconut and stir it around the hot pan until the coconut smells aromatic. (If using fresh coconut, sauté it in a separate pan.) Leave to cool, then transfer to a food processor and blend with a splash of water to a coarse or smooth paste, as desired. Set aside.

Rinse the aubergines under running water, then with a sharp knife cut each aubergine into quarters, from botttom to top but keeping the stem end intact. Place in a large bowl, cover with water and ½ teaspoon of the salt. Leave to soak for 10–15 minutes.

Heat the oil in a pan (that has a lid) over a medium heat. Drain the aubergines and wipe dry with paper towels, then add to the hot oil. Fry, turning regularly, until the skins are blistered all over, then remove from the oil and set aside.

Pour away some of the hot oil, keeping 2 tablespoons in the pan. Add the cumin, mustard and onion seeds. When they begin to crackle, add the onions and curry leaves, and sprinkle with the remaining ½ teaspoon of salt. Fry until the onions are translucent, then add the ginger-garlic paste and fry until the raw smell goes away. Pour the measured water into the pan, then add the peanut-coconut paste, red chilli powder, garam masala, ground coriander and turmeric. Cook, stirring, for 8–10 minutes. Stir in the tamarind paste, bring to the boil, then stir in the fried aubergines and asafoetida. Add more water, if needed, to bring the gravy to a semi-thick consistency. Cover and cook until the aubergine is completely cooked through.

Serve garnished with the chopped coriander leaves, with biryani, pulao or roti.

HYDERABADI VEGETABLE DUM BIRYANI

Hyderabadi biryani is a style of biryani originating in the kitchens of the former *nizams* (rulers) of Hyderabad State and is a key dish in the region's cusine. It is traditionally made with basmati rice and meat (mostly mutton), but there are a lot of variations to be found with seasonal greens and mushrooms. Hyderabad is particularly famous for its biryani and kababs. I have tried many biryanis over the years, but my personal favourite is definitely Hyderabadi, which is normally served with raita.

Serves 4

100ml/3½fl oz/scant ½ cup warm milk
½ tsp saffron strands
2 tbsp ghee, for frying, plus 2 tbsp for layering the biryani
2 tbsp rapeseed/canola oil
200g/7oz onions, sliced
80g/3oz red bell pepper/capsicum, cubed
100g/3½oz crispy fried onions (can be store-bought)
2 tbsp chopped fresh coriander
4 tbsp chopped fresh mint
1 tsp Biryani Masala (see page 16)
1 tbsp rose water
1 tbsp dried rose petals

MARINADE
250g/9oz/1 cup plain yogurt
2 tbsp Ginger-Garlic Paste (see page 17)
2 green chillies, chopped
2 tsp lemon juice
2 tsp rapeseed/canola oil
2 tbsp Garam Masala (store-bought or see page 12)
1 tsp coarsely ground black pepper
1 tsp chilli powder
1 tsp ground coriander
1 tsp salt
½ tsp ground turmeric

VEGETABLE MIXTURE
150g/5oz potatoes, parboiled and cubed
50g/1¾oz green beans, diced
80g/3oz carrots, cubed
50g/1¾oz/⅓ cup green peas
10 portobello mushrooms, diced
3 tbsp chopped fresh mint
3 tbsp chopped fresh coriander/cilantro

RICE
450g/1lb/2¼ cups basmati rice
2 bay leaves
4 black cardamom pods
5cm/2in cinnamon stick
4 green cardamom pods
5–6 cloves
2 tbsp ground coriander
3 green chillies, slit
2 tbsp salt
2 tsp lemon juice
1 tsp ghee

Infuse the warm milk with the saffron strands and set aside.

Mix together the ingredients for the marinade in a large bowl. Add the vegetable mixture to the marinade and mix well, then cover and leave to marinate for 30 minutes.

At the same time, rinse the basmati rice under cold running water until the water runs clear, then place the rice in a bowl, cover with fresh water and leave to soak for 30 minutes.

In a large, heavy pan heat the ghee for frying and the oil over a medium heat, then add the onions and fry until golden brown. Add the bell pepper chunks and fry until soft but still with a bit of crunch, then add the marinated vegetable mixture and mix well. Cover and cook for 10 minutes, or until the vegetables are almost cooked. Set aside.

Drain the soaked rice. Fill a large pan with water and add all the other rice ingredients. Boil for 5 minutes, or until the water turns flavourful, then add the rice and mix gently. Bring back to the boil and cook for 5 minutes, or until the rice is almost cooked. Drain well.

To layer the biryani, take a large kadai or casserole dish and spread the vegetable mixture over the base. Top with half of each of the fried onions, chopped coriander and mint. Top this layer with the cooked rice and level out uniformly. Top the rice with the remaining fried onions, coriander and mint. Pour over the saffron milk, biryani masala, rose water, dried rose petals and remaining ghee.

Cover tightly with kitchen foil and place the lid on the dish. Place over a medium heat and simmer for 20 minutes, or until the rice is well cooked.

Leave to rest, still covered, for at least 30 minutes before serving with raita.

Option You can make chicken or mutton biryani following the same recipe replacing the vegetable mix with 750g/1lb 10oz meat. You can also play around with the spice level, increasing or decreasing the amount of chilli powder and fresh green chillies according to taste.

ANDHRA LAMB MASALA

A delicacy of Andhra cuisine, this knockout recipe is a spicy and delicious fry that can be served with rice or chapati. It is very simple and easy to prepare with basic ingredients that are likely readily available in your kitchen.

Serves 4

500g/1lb 2oz lamb or mutton, diced into bite-size chunks
1 tsp salt, or to taste
¼ tsp ground turmeric
150ml/5fl oz/⅔ cup rapeseed/canola oil, for frying
8–10 fresh curry leaves
200g/7oz onions, chopped
1 tsp Ginger-Garlic Paste (see page 17)
100g/3½oz fresh or canned tomatoes, chopped
½ tsp Kashmiri chilli powder
200ml/7fl oz/scant 1 cup water
2 tsp freshly ground black pepper
fresh coriander/cilantro leaves, to garnish

SPICE MIX

1 tsp coriander seeds
1 tsp cumin seeds
1 tsp poppy seeds
½ tsp fennel seeds
5cm/2in cinnamon stick
2 cloves
2 green cardamom pods
4 black peppercorns

Place the lamb or mutton pieces in a bowl, add the salt and turmeric and toss well to coat. Set aside.

Dry-roast the spices for the spice mix in a kadai or heavy saucepan until aromatic. Leave to cool, then grind them to a fine powder in a spice grinder.

Heat the oil in a large pan over a medium heat. Once hot, add the curry leaves, then add the onions and sauté until the onions are brown. Add the marinated meat pieces and cook over a high heat until well seared. Add the ginger-garlic paste and cook until the raw smell goes away, then add the tomatoes and cook over a high heat until the tomatoes are soft. Add the spice mix and chilli powder, and cook over a medium heat for 10–15 minutes.

When the masala coats the meat pieces and they start to look dry, add the measured water and bring to the boil. Simmer rapidly until the water evaporates, leaving a nice thick gravy. Continue to cook until the oil starts to separate from the gravy and the meat is cooked through. Once the water is completely gone, each piece of meat will have a nice coating of sauce around it. Add the freshly ground black pepper and stir well.

Serve, garnished with coriander leaves.

EGG KURMA

Egg curries are very popular across India and every single region has their own way of preparing them. In North India, this mild dish is referred to as *korma* and is made with a base of yogurt and cashew nuts. In South India, it is *kurma* and is made with coconut as the base. Being Punjabi, I was naturally serving a Punjabi egg curry recipe at my restaurant Manthan in Mayfair, but I recently changed to this South Indian version as I find it very well balanced.

Serves 4

100ml/3½fl oz/scant ½ cup cooking oil
2 small bay leaves
1 cinnamon stick, about 5cm/2in long
4 green cardamom pods
1 tsp caraway seeds
300g/10½oz onions, finely chopped
2 tbsp Ginger-Garlic Paste (see page 17)
200g/7oz fresh or canned tomatoes, roughly chopped
1 tsp ground turmeric
1 tsp salt, or to taste
4 green chillies, slit
1 tsp red chilli powder
2 tsp ground coriander
1 tsp fennel seeds, roasted and ground
16–20 curry leaves
8 eggs, soft-boiled and peeled
1 tsp Garam Masala (store-bought or see page 12)

POPPY SEED & COCONUT MILK PASTE

8 tbsp poppy seeds
200ml/7fl oz/scant 1 cup coconut milk

First, make the poppy seed and coconut milk paste. Add the poppy seeds and coconut milk to a blender and blitz to a smooth, thick paste. Set aside.

Heat the oil in a large pan over a medium heat. Once hot, add the bay leaves, cinnamon stick, cardamom pods and caraway seeds. Sauté until they begin to crackle, then add the onions and sauté until golden.

Add the ginger-garlic paste and sauté until the raw smell goes away, then add the chopped tomatoes, turmeric and salt, and cook until the tomatoes are soft. Add the fresh green chillies, chilli powder, ground coriander and fennel seeds, and cook until fragrant, then add the poppy seed and coconut milk paste, and cook until that too is fragrant. Add the curry leaves and cook for 1 minute.

Add just enough water to the pan to make a thick gravy of the sauce and simmer until it thickens slightly but not too much. Prick the boiled eggs a few times with a fork and add them to the gravy. Cook the eggs in the gravy until you can see traces of oil starting to pool on the top. (As an option, you can also fry the eggs in 2 tsp ghee, then add to the *kurma*.)

Add the garam masala, mix well, then remove from the heat and serve with plain rice or paratha.

KHATTI DAL

Hailing from nearby Hyderabad, this is a simple dal recipe with a perfect balance of flavours. South Indians add tamarind and tomatoes to their dishes, which bring a tangy sourness that works so well. This goes beautifully with plain rice, raita and pappadums. I use toor dal (yellow lentils) here, but you can also use masoor dal (red lentils) to make this.

Serves 4

- 200g/7oz/1 cup plus 2 tbsp toor dal/yellow lentils, rinsed and drained
- 70g/2½oz tomatoes, finely chopped
- 1 tsp finely chopped fresh garlic
- 1 tsp finely chopped fresh root ginger
- 1 tsp finely chopped green chillies
- ½ tsp ground turmeric
- ½ tsp red chilli powder
- 1 tsp salt, or to taste
- 500ml/17fl oz/2 cups water
- 1 tbsp tamarind paste
- fresh coriander/cilantro leaves, to garnish

TADKA

- 1 tbsp rapeseed/canola oil
- 1 tsp mustard seeds
- 1 tsp cumin seeds
- 3 garlic cloves, sliced
- 8–10 curry leaves
- 2 dried red chillies
- 1 tbsp chopped fresh coriander/cilantro leaves

In a large, deep pan, combine the washed dal with the chopped tomatoes, garlic, ginger, green chillies, turmeric, chilli powder, salt and measured water. Cook over a medium heat for 10–15 minutes, or until the lentils are soft (the lentils may need a further 5–10 minutes if they are not ready yet).

Thoroughly stir the cooked dal until smooth, add the tamarind paste and bring the mixture to a brisk boil, then reduce to a simmer.

In a small pan, heat the oil for the *tadka* over a medium heat. Add the mustard and cumin seeds, allow to crackle, then add the sliced garlic and fry until golden brown. Add the curry leaves and dried chillies, and fry for another few seconds.

Pour the *tadka* over the dal and simmer for a further 4–5 minutes. Check the seasoning and adjust to your taste.

Serve garnished with coriander leaves, with some rice and pappadums.

HALEEM

This flavourful mutton stew is widely consumed over a large region, stretching from South to Central Asia and encompassing the Middle East. It is served both as a street food and also as a celebration dish during Ramadan. It varies from region to region, but usually includes wheat or barley, meat and lentils. Enjoy with flatbreads or on its own.

Serves 4

80g/3oz/½ cup bulgur wheat
3 tbsp urad dal
3 tbsp toor dal
2 tbsp yellow moong dal
3 tbsp chana dal
100ml/3½fl oz/scant ½ cup rapeseed/canola oil
150g/5oz onions, thinly sliced
500g/1lb 2oz boneless mutton, trimmed and cut into bite-size pieces
2 litres/70fl oz/8½ cups water
2 tsp Ginger-Garlic Paste (see page 17)
½ tsp salt, or to taste
1 tsp Kashmiri chilli powder
¼ tsp ground turmeric
4 green chillies, slit
½ tsp black peppercorns
100g/3½oz ghee
2 bay leaves
4 green cardamom pods
2 black cardamom pods
2.5cm/1in cinnamon stick
30g/1oz fresh coriander/cilantro leaves, chopped
150g/5oz/generous ½ cup plain yogurt
1 tbsp ground coriander
1 tsp Garam Masala (store-bought or see page 12)
2–3 lime wedges
30g/1oz fresh mint, chopped

Put the bulgur wheat in twice the amount of water and leave to soak. Simultaneously, soak the lentils in a separate bowl.

Heat the oil in a frying pan over a medium-low heat. Fry the onions until golden brown. Remove with a slotted spoon and set aside.

Place the mutton in a heavy pan along with 1 litre/35fl oz/4¼ cups of the water. Bring to the boil, then reduce to a simmer and cook for 30–40 minutes.

After this time, add 1 teaspoon of the ginger-garlic paste, the salt, chilli powder and ⅛ teaspoon of the ground turmeric. Simmer for another 15–20 minutes, then remove from the heat. Shred the meat and set aside. If there is any liquid left in the pan, drain it off and reserve for later.

Drain the bulgur and lentils. Add to the pan along with the remaining teaspoon of ginger-garlic paste, ⅛ teaspoon turmeric, 2 slit green chillies and the peppercorns. Add 300ml/10fl oz/1¼ cups water and bring to the boil. Simmer until the bulgur and lentils are soft and the water absorbed. Transfer the mixture to a blender and blitz for a few seconds.

Heat 50g/1¾oz of the ghee in the heavy pan over a medium heat, add the bay leaves, cardamom pods and cinnamon stick, and stir well. Add the shredded lamb, 2 remaining green chillies and half of the fresh coriander. Sauté for 2–3 minutes. Add the yogurt, ground coriander and garam masala, and cook for 10–15 minutes.

Add the remaining 700ml/24fl oz/3 cups of water and bring to the boil, then add the bulgur wheat mixture and the remaining ghee. Mix well, then reduce to a simmer for 30 minutes.

Serve hot, garnished with the fried onions, lime wedges, mint leaves and the remaining fresh coriander.

DOUBLE KA MEETHA

This is one of the easiest desserts to make, although it does take some time. Hailing from the palace kitchens of the Hyderabad royal family, it is very similar to bread and butter pudding. It is worth the time taken to make it, because it just tastes so good.

Serves 4

1 litre/35fl oz/4¼ cups whole/full-fat milk
200ml/7fl oz/scant 1 cup condensed milk
¼ tsp saffron strands
½ tsp ground cardamom
300g/10½oz ghee
10 white bread slices, halved diagonally
200g/7oz/1 cup white granulated sugar
250ml/9fl oz/1 cup water

TOPPING
10–12 skin-on almonds, roughly chopped
10–12 cashews, roughly chopped
2 tsp ghee

TO DECORATE
dried rose petals
slivered pistachios

Heat the milk in a non-stick pan over a medium-high heat, stirring constantly to avoid scorching. Once the milk comes to the boil, reduce the heat to medium-low and add the condensed milk and saffron. Cook for about 1 hour, stirring frequently, until the milk is thick and has reduced by half. Stir in the ground cardamom and set aside.

Heat the ghee in a deep frying pan over a medium heat. When hot, fry the bread slices on both sides until just lightly browned (you will need to work in batches). Remove to a plate lined with paper towels.

Combine the sugar and measured water in a saucepan and bring to the boil over a medium-high heat, stirring regularly. Cook for 6–8 minutes until the syrup has thickened slightly. Remove from the heat and set aside.

To make the topping, mix the almonds and cashews with the ghee and set aside.

Preheat the oven to 180°C/160°C fan/350°F/Gas 4.

In an oven-safe baking dish, arrange the crispy bread slices over the base. Pour over the sugar syrup, then pour over the thickened milk mixture. Sprinkle over the topping. Bake in the middle of the oven for 20–25 minutes until slightly browned on top.

Cool slightly before decorating with dried rose petals and slivered pistachios. Either serve warm or chill for a few hours before serving.

ANDHRA PRADESH

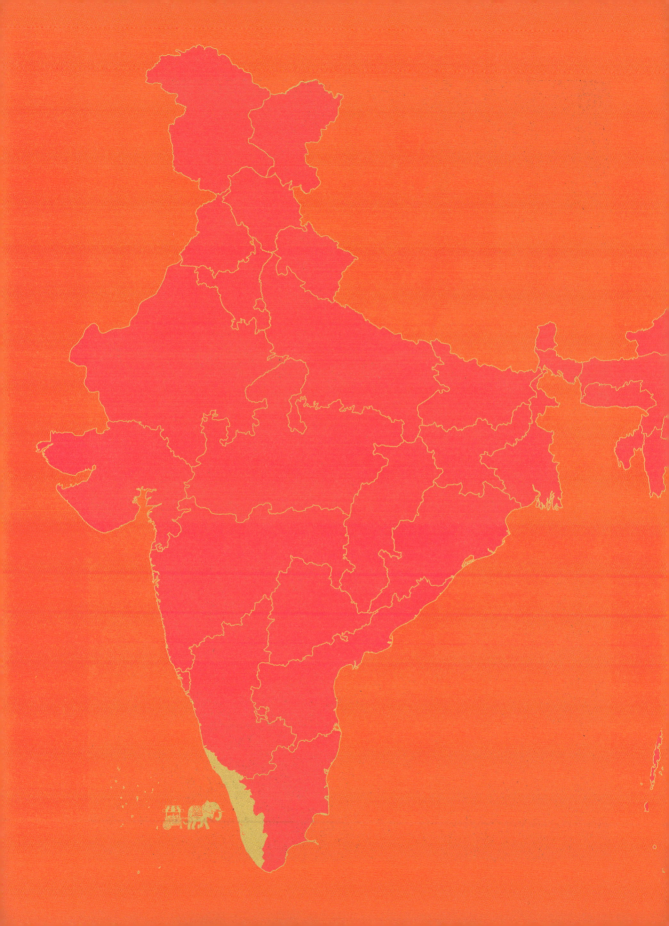

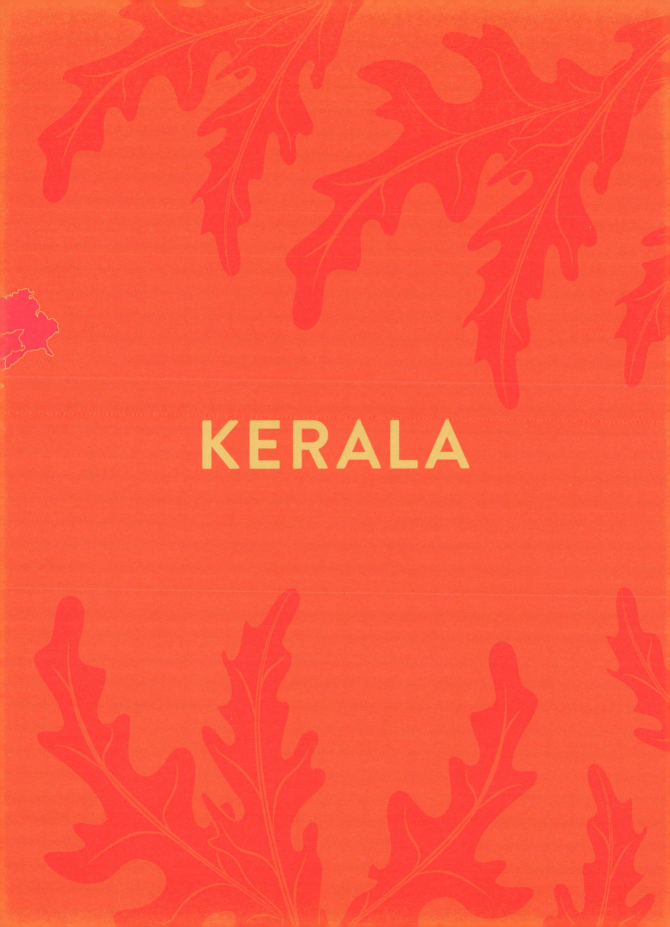

KERALA

KERALA

Kerala is a state on the south-western Malabar coast of India, and its cuisine offers up a multitude of dishes unique to the region. As an important trading hub for spices, the region naturally attracted visitors from all over the world. Those who settled in the local area brought with them new cooking techniques and ingredients, and over time these were absorbed into the local repetoire, making Keralan cuisine quite unique from others in India. Being coastal, coconuts abound, as does seafood, and these both feature abundantly, as well as a variety of spicy meat dishes (due to the prominent Christian communities, it is one of the few regions in India where beef is eaten).

In addition to the heavy use of coconut products, fresh chillies provide heat, and spices are delicate: mustard seeds, cardamom, turmeric and asafoetida are frequently used. Tamarind is a common souring agent. Rice is the typical accompaniment to most dishes, although parathas are also favoured, along with *appam* – a *dosa*-like pancake. When visiting the region, you might expect to be offered a *sadya* – a vegetarian feast typically encompassing up to 28 different dishes at a time – rice, savouries, side dishes, poppadums, pickles and desserts – that is usually served on a large plantain leaf. It is a delicious experience.

Don't miss the Banana Leaf Fish (page 134), Keralan Fish Curry (page 144), *Nadan* Beef (page 138) and Cabbage *Thoran* (page 137). *Payasams* (sweet milk puddings) are another regional favourite – do try *Semiyan Payasam* (Vermicelli Kheer – page 148).

KARIMEEN POLLICHATHU (Banana Leaf Fish)

A fantastic, flavourful recipe, also known as *Meen Pollichathu*, this Keralan dish is a popular street food offering. Everywhere you go in South India, you will find small roadside vendors cooking fish, marinated in coconut oil and spices, wrapped in banana leaves. Be aware – it has a good amount of chilli in it, as Keralans prefer it slightly on the hotter side.

Serves 4

- 4 sea bass or bream fillets
- ½ tsp ground turmeric
- ½ tsp freshly ground black pepper
- 1 tsp ground coriander
- ½ tsp chilli powder
- 100ml/3½fl oz/scant ½ cup vegetable oil
- ½ tsp black mustard seeds
- a few curry leaves
- 100g/3½oz shallots, finely sliced
- 2–3 green chillies, slit
- 1 tbsp finely chopped garlic
- 50g/1¾oz tomatoes, finely chopped
- 1 tsp coconut vinegar or white wine vinegar
- 1½ tbsp coconut cream
- 4 banana leaves, for cooking (optional – you can also use pieces of kitchen foil)
- 1 tbsp chopped fresh coriander/cilantro
- salt, to taste

On a plate, rub the fish fillets all over with half of the turmeric and black pepper along with a good pinch of salt. Set aside for 20 minutes or so, to marinate.

In a small bowl, combine the ground coriander, chilli powder, remaining turmeric, black pepper and another ¼ teaspoon salt with just enough water to create a paste. Set aside.

Preheat the oven to 220°C/200°C fan/425°F/Gas 7 and place a baking sheet inside to get hot.

Heat half of the oil in a frying pan over a medium heat. When hot, add the black mustard seeds. As soon as they start to pop, add the curry leaves. Fry for a moment, then add the shallots and sauté until translucent. Add the spice paste, chillies and chopped garlic. Fry gently for about 30 seconds, then add the tomatoes and vinegar. Cook for a few minutes until the tomatoes have largely broken down, then stir in the coconut cream. Simmer over a medium heat for 5 minutes, or until most of the moisture has evaporated and you have a thick masala paste. Remove from the heat and leave to cool.

Heat the remaining oil in another frying pan. Fry the fish for 1 minute on each side, lightly browning the skin. Leave to cool.

Grease the banana leaves (or kitchen foil) with a little oil (this can be the same oil you used to fry the fish). Apply a thick layer of the masala paste to one side of each fish fillet, pressing it in well. Place the fillets, coated-side down, on each banana leaf (or piece of foil). Coat the other side of the fillets in the paste, then wrap each up tightly. If using banana leaves, it helps to additionally wrap each parcel in a layer of foil to hold them together. Place on the hot baking sheet and bake for 10–12 minutes.

Remove from the oven and open the parcels. Check the seasoning and sprinkle with the fresh coriander. Serve with lime wedges and plain rice.

CABBAGE THORAN

This simple, quick and tasty dish is very common in Keralan cuisine. It is also an important dish for the festival of Sadya (part of Kerala's harvest festival, Onam). Shredded cabbage is simply cooked in coconut oil, tempered with spices and curry leaves, and finished with a good amount of freshly grated coconut. It can be served as a main with flatbreads, or as a side dish.

Serves 4

500g/1lb 2oz cabbage
3 tbsp coconut oil
1 tsp mustard seeds
1 tsp cumin seeds
100g/3½oz shallots, finely chopped
1 green chilli, finely chopped
10–12 curry leaves
½ tsp ground turmeric
pinch of asafoetida
2 tbsp chopped fresh root ginger
pinch of salt, or to taste
50g/1¾oz freshly grated coconut
2 tablespoons chopped fresh coriander/cilantro leaves, to garnish

Rinse the cabbage a few times in fresh water, then remove the outer leaves. Cut in half or into quarters, then thinly shred. Set aside.

In a heavy pan (that has a lid), heat the coconut oil over a medium heat. When hot, add the mustard seeds and sauté over a low heat until they crackle. Add the cumin seeds and sauté until they change colour, then add the chopped shallots and sauté, stirring often, until translucent. Add the green chilli and curry leaves, and sauté for a minute, then stir in the ground turmeric and asafoetida. Add the cabbage along with the chopped ginger and salt, stir well and sauté for a minute. Cover and cook over a low heat for 8–10 minutes, stirring occasionally, until the cabbage is tender.

Remove the pan lid. If there is any moisture left in the pan, cook until it has all evaporated, then add the freshly grated coconut. Stir well and cook for a final 2–3 minutes.

Serve hot, garnished with chopped coriander, with chapatis or as a side dish.

NADAN BEEF

This spicy beef fry is a traditional Keralan dish. The meat is slow-cooked with typical South Indian spices until tender and is then fried again in a mix of onions and spices until each morsel of meat gets a caramelized coating of the spicy gravy. It is usually served with flatbreads as a main, but it also goes very well with drinks as an appetizer or starter.

Serves 4

750g/1lb 10oz boneless beef shin or shoulder, cut into 2.5cm/1in chunks
½ tsp ground turmeric
2 tbsp ground coriander
250g/9oz onions, finely chopped
1 tbsp finely chopped fresh root ginger
1 tbsp finely chopped garlic
4–5 green chillies, slit
100g/3½oz fresh coconut pieces/chips
10–15 curry leaves
200ml/7fl oz/scant 1 cup water, or as needed
100ml/3½fl oz/scant ½ cup vegetable oil
15–20 pearl onions, peeled but left whole
1 tbsp coconut oil (optional)
salt, to taste

SPICE MIX

2 tsp fennel seeds
1 tsp black peppercorns
4 green cardamom pods
4 cloves
2 x 5cm/2in cinnamon sticks
1 star anise
1 tsp cumin seeds

In a large frying pan, dry-roast all the spices for the spice mix for 3–4 minutes until fragrant. Leave to cool, then transfer to a spice grinder or pestle and mortar and grind to a fine powder. Set aside.

Place the beef in a large bowl and add 2 teaspoons of the ground spice mix along with the ground turmeric, 1 tablespoon of the ground coriander, chopped onions, ginger, garlic, green chillies, coconut pieces, half of the curry leaves and 1 teaspoon of salt. Turn until well mixed and the beef is well coated and leave to marinate for 20–30 minutes.

Transfer the beef mixture to a large pan, add the measured water and cook over a low heat, stirring occasionally, for 20–30 minutes, adding more water if the pan starts to look dry before the beef is cooked.

In a separate large, heavy pan (that has a lid), heat the vegetable oil over a medium heat. When hot, add the pearl onions and remaining curry leaves and sauté until browned. Add the remaining ground spice mix along with the remaining ground coriander and sauté for 2 minutes. Add the cooked beef along with its cooking juices, bring to the boil, then reduce the heat to its lowest. Cover and cook for 20–30 minutes.

Remove the lid and continue to cook until the beef becomes darker in colour – this might take a further 8–10 minutes. If the pan starts to look too dry, add a tablespoon or so of water from time to time. If using, you can also add coconut oil at this point, as it will intensify the flavour of the dish. When the beef is nicely roasted and very dark in colour, it's ready.

Serve hot with chapatis, or on its own as a starter.

KERALA

KERALAN VEGETABLE STEW

A popular choice for vegetarians from South India, this healthy stew is often served for breakfast with *appam* (also know as hoppers – lacy rice pancakes) or *dosa* (savoury gram flour crêpes), but it can just as easily be served throughout the day. It is a delicious combination of seasonal greens and coconut milk finished with South Indian spices, and is very quick to make.

Serves 4

100ml/3½fl oz/scant ½ cup rapeseed/canola oil
6 cloves
5cm/2in cinnamon stick
6 green cardamom pods
150g/5oz onions, thinly sliced
20 French beans, cut into batons
100g/3½oz carrots, diced
100g/3½oz potatoes, peeled and cubed
100g/3½oz green peas or frozen peas
150g/5oz cauliflower florets
6 green chillies, slit
1 tbsp julienned fresh root ginger
150ml/5fl oz/⅔ cup water
1 tsp salt, or to taste
4–6 curry leaves
600ml/20fl oz/2½ cups coconut milk
½ tsp coarsely ground black pepper

In a large pan (that has a lid), heat the oil over a medium heat. When hot, add the cloves, cinnamon stick and cardamom pods, and sauté for about 30 seconds. Add the sliced onions and sauté until they shrink slightly but do not brown. Add the French beans, diced carrots, cubed potatoes, peas, cauliflower florets, green chillies and ginger, and sauté for 1 minute. Add the measured water, salt and half the curry leaves, and mix well. Cover and cook for 5 minutes, or until the vegetables are half cooked.

Add the coconut milk to the stew and mix well. Cook for a further 8–10 minutes until all the vegetables are cooked through. Remove from the heat, stir in the remaining curry leaves and ground pepper, then check the seasoning, adding more salt if needed.

Serve as a side dish to other mains, or as a main with paratha.

NADAN KOZHI

Kerala's home-style chicken curry, *Nadan Kozhi* is balanced, rich and aromatic, and bursting with the South Indian flavours of curry leaves, black pepper, fennel and creamy coconut.

Serves 4

- 100ml/3½fl oz/scant ½ cup vegetable oil
- 1 tsp black mustard seeds
- 1 tsp fennel seeds
- 10 curry leaves
- 150g/5oz onions, finely chopped
- 1 tbsp salt
- 3 garlic cloves, crushed
- 1 tbsp freshly grated root ginger
- 1 tsp freshly ground black pepper
- 1 tsp ground turmeric
- 2 tsp Kashmiri chilli powder
- 1 tsp Garam Masala (store-bought or see page 12)
- 750g/1lb 10oz boneless, skinless chicken thighs (about 8–10), each cut into 3 generous chunks
- 200g/7oz tomato purée/tomato concentrate
- 125ml/4fl oz/½ cup water
- 100ml/3½fl oz/scant ½ cup coconut milk

Heat the oil in a large pan (that has a lid) over a medium heat. When hot, add the mustard seeds, fennel seeds and curry leaves. As soon as the mustard seeds start to pop, add the chopped onions and salt, and sauté until the onions soften, about 8–10 minutes. Add the garlic, ginger and remaining spices, and sauté for a couple of minutes until fragrant. Stir in the chicken pieces to evenly coat them with the spicy onion mixture and cook for 5 minutes, stirring occasionally. Stir in the tomato purée and measured water, cover and cook for 30 minutes at a gentle simmer.

Check the chicken pieces are thoroughly cooked and not pink in the middle, then pour in the coconut milk and stir until fully incorporated and heated through.

Serve with basmati rice or roti.

VARUTHARACHA MUTTON CURRY

This is one of the most famous traditional dishes in Kerala. Simple, delicious and spicy, it's a never-fail recipe that works just as well with lamb or chicken as with mutton.

Serves 4

300ml/10½fl oz/1¼ cups water, plus 2 tbsp
500g/1lb 2oz boneless mutton or lamb, cut into 5cm/2in chunks
½ tsp ground turmeric
50g/1¾oz/generous ½ cup desiccated/dried shredded or grated fresh coconut
1 tsp black peppercorns
100ml/3½fl oz/scant ½ cup rapeseed/canola oil
1 bay leaf
2 green cardamom pods
2 cloves
2 x 2.5cm/1in cinnamon sticks
½ tsp finely chopped fresh root ginger
5–6 garlic cloves, chopped
200g/7oz onions, thinly sliced
2–3 green chillies, slit
1 tbsp ground coriander
1 tsp Kashmiri chilli powder
½ tsp Garam Masala (store-bought or see page 12)
½ tsp ground fennel
100g/3½oz tomatoes, chopped
salt, to taste

TEMPERING

2 tbsp rapeseed/canola oil
½ tsp mustard seeds
3 tbsp thinly sliced fresh coconut
1 sprig of curry leaves

Heat the 300ml/10½ fl oz/1¼ cups water in a deep pan over a medium heat, add the mutton pieces along with the turmeric and 1 teaspoon salt. Simmer for 20–25 minutes until the mutton is just done. Separate the mutton pieces from the stock and set both aside.

Dry-roast the coconut in a frying pan until it turns brown, then remove from the heat, add the black peppercorns and swirl to heat briefly. Transfer to a pestle and mortar and grind to a smooth paste (do not add any water). Set aside.

Heat the oil in a large pan (that has a lid) over a medium heat. When hot, add the bay leaf, cardamom pods, cloves and cinnamon sticks, and sauté for a few seconds. Add the ginger, garlic, onions, green chillies and 1 teaspoon salt, and sauté for about 10–15 minutes until the onions are golden brown.

Reduce the heat to low and add the ground spices along with the 2 tablespoons of water. Sauté for about 5 minutes, then add the cooked mutton pieces and mix until well combined. Add the coconut paste, chopped tomatoes and 300ml/10½fl oz/1¼ cups of the reserved stock. Taste and adjust the salt level at this point. Cover and cook over a medium heat for about 10–12 minutes, or until the gravy is nice and thick.

For the tempering, heat the oil in a small pan over a medium heat. When hot, add the mustard seeds and let splutter, then add the coconut and curry leaves. Sauté until the coconut is golden brown, then remove from the heat.

Pour the tempering mixture over the curry and serve.

KERALA

KERALAN FISH CURRY

Originating from the tropical south coast of India, Keralan-style fish curries often feature creamy coconut milk. I like to serve this with plain rice or chapatis. *Pictured overleaf (right).*

Serves 4

rapeseed/canola oil, for frying
2 tsp mustard seeds
1 tsp fenugreek seeds
16–20 curry leaves
500g/1lb 2oz onions, finely sliced
2 tbsp Ginger-Garlic Paste (see page 17)
16 dried kokum (black mangosteen) (or 2 tbsp tamarind pulp as a substitute)
2 tsp red chilli powder
4 tsp ground coriander
pinch of ground turmeric
300g/10½oz fresh tomatoes, sliced
50g/1¾oz fresh root ginger, julienned
8 green chillies, slit
800ml/28fl oz/scant 3½ cups coconut milk
4 sea bass fillets (300–400g/10½–14oz each) (any other white fish will also work)
salt, to taste

To make the sauce, heat a splash of oil in a pan. When hot, add the mustard seeds, fenugreek seeds and curry leaves, and stir until they start to crackle. Add the onions and cook over a medium heat for about 5 minutes until golden brown. Add the ginger-garlic paste and cook for another 3–4 minutes.

Add the kokum (or tamarind pulp), red chilli powder, ground coriander and turmeric, and stir for 1 minute, then add the tomatoes, ginger and green chillies. Cook over a low heat until the tomatoes are mushy and soft.

Add the coconut milk and continue to cook over a low heat for 10–15 minutes.

Meanwhile, season the sea bass fillets with salt. Heat a splash of oil in a non-stick frying pan over a medium heat. Add the fish to the pan, skin-side down, and fry for 4–6 minutes, or until the skin is crisp (no need to turn the fish).

When you're ready to serve, reheat the sauce (if needed), then divide among serving dishes and top with the crispy fish fillets.

THAYIR SADAM

Curd rice is a traditional Keralan dish made with precooked rice, yogurt (curd), herbs and tempering spices. It is usually eaten year-round as a part of a meal rather than as a standalone dish. As well as being gut-healthy, curd rice is also a comforting summer food that keeps the body cool. Everyone has their own favourite way of enjoying curd rice, and this is mine. *Pictured overleaf (left).*

Serves 4

125g/4½oz/½ cup rice (can use equal parts white rice and brown rice, if wished)
350ml/12fl oz/1½ cups water
50ml/1¾fl oz/scant ¼ cup milk (optional)
375g/13¼oz/1½ cups plain yogurt, plus extra if needed
1 tsp finely chopped fresh coriander/cilantro leaves (optional)
2 tbsp grated carrot
2 tbsp grated cucumber
salt, to taste
pomegranate seeds, to garnish

TEMPERING
1 tsp neutral oil
½ tsp mustard seeds
½ tsp cumin seeds (optional)
1 dried red chilli, broken
¾–1 tsp chana dal (optional)
¾–1 tsp urad dal (optional)
6–8 roasted cashews, split or chopped (optional)
½ tsp minced fresh root ginger
1 green chilli, slit or chopped (optional)
1 sprig of curry leaves
pinch of asafoetida

Rinse the rice a few times until the water runs clear, then drain. Transfer the rice to a large pan (that has a lid), add the measured water and ½ teaspoon of salt and bring to the boil. Reduce to a simmer and cook for 10–15 minutes, or until all the water has been absorbed.

Mash the rice lightly (or simply fluff it up and use as is, if you do not like mushy rice). If you are not planning to serve the rice immediately, you can stir in the milk (this helps to keep the rice fresh for a few hours). Leave to cool completely.

When the rice is completely cooled, add the yogurt and mix well until combined. Stir in the coriander, if using, along with the grated carrot and cucumber. Taste and add more salt, if needed.

To finish, heat the oil for the tempering in a small pan. Add the mustard seeds and cumin seeds, if using, and when they begin to splutter add the red chilli, chana dal, urad dal and cashews, if using. Fry until the dal turns golden. Add the ginger, green chilli (if using) and curry leaves, then when the curry leaves have turned crisp, add the asafoetida and remove from the heat.

Pour the tempering into the curd rice and mix to combine.

Serve garnished with pomegranate seeds.

SEMIYAN PAYASAM

Semiyan payasam is a South Indian sweet made with vermicelli noodles, milk, ghee, sugar or jaggery, raisins and nuts. It is one of the easiest desserts to make and is ready in under 20 minutes. I personally prefer to make this with coconut milk rather than dairy milk, and jaggery rather than sugar, for the added nutrients. For a fully dairy-free option swap the ghee out for rapeseed/canola oil.

Serves 4

2 tbsp ghee
12–15 cashews
8–10 raisins
200g/7oz thick vermicelli noodles (semiyan)
600ml/20fl oz/2½ cups coconut milk
100g/3½oz/scant ½ cup jaggery or granulated sugar
½ tsp ground cardamom
50g/1¾oz fresh coconut, grated
a few saffron strands
50g/1¾oz mix of fresh berries, to serve

Heat 1 tablespoon of the ghee in a heavy pan over a medium heat. Add the cashews and sauté until golden, then add the raisins and sauté just until they plump up. Remove to a plate and set aside.

Add the other tablespoon of ghee and the vermicelli noodles to the same pan and sauté over a low–medium heat until golden. Add the milk and slowly bring to the boil over a medium heat. Boil until the vermicelli is fully cooked (check the package instructions) and keep stirring to avoid burning.

Add the jaggery or sugar to the pan and simmer over a low heat for 3–5 minutes until the mixture becomes thick. Stir in the ground cardamom, grated coconut and saffron, and remove from the heat when the mixture reaches a thick pouring consistency. It will thicken further after cooling.

Serve hot or chilled as desired, divided among bowls and decorated with the fried nuts and raisins, and assorted fresh berries.

NEER MOR

Buttermilk is a popular non-alcoholic, yogurt-based drink, which has many variations throughout India. This version is a simple buttermilk made from yogurt and water, which is spiced and then tempered too. It's very refreshing, simple and easy to make with limited ingredients. A wonderful summer drink to serve with a meal, I prefer to drink it chilled, so I always add few ice cubes too. You can find this drink at my restaurants where everyone loves it. If you don't like it spicy, omit the green chilli.

Serves 4

250g/9oz/1 cup plain yogurt
1 tsp finely chopped fresh root ginger
1 tsp finely chopped green chilli (omit if you prefer it non-spicy)
200ml/7fl oz/scant 1 cup water, or as needed
2 tbsp finely chopped fresh coriander/cilantro
salt, to taste
ice cubes, to serve (optional)

TEMPERING
1 tsp rapeseed/canola oil
½ tsp mustard seeds
6–7 curry leaves, chopped
small pinch of asafoetida

In a blender or food processor, combine the yogurt, ginger, green chilli and a pinch of salt. Add the measured water and blend thoroughly (if you want to add ice to chill it to serving temperature immediately, reduce the water and add some ice now). You may have some butter floating on the top of the mixture, but this is fine and tastes good.

Pour the spiced buttermilk mixture into a bowl or jug and add the chopped coriander. Mix well and set aside.

Heat the oil for the tempering in a small pan over a medium heat. When hot, reduce the heat, add the mustard seeds and chopped curry leaves. Once they crackle, add the asafoetida, mix well and quickly remove from the heat.

Pour the tempering mixture into the buttermilk and mix well.

Either serve immediately, over ice (if wished), or chill in the refrigerator to serve later.

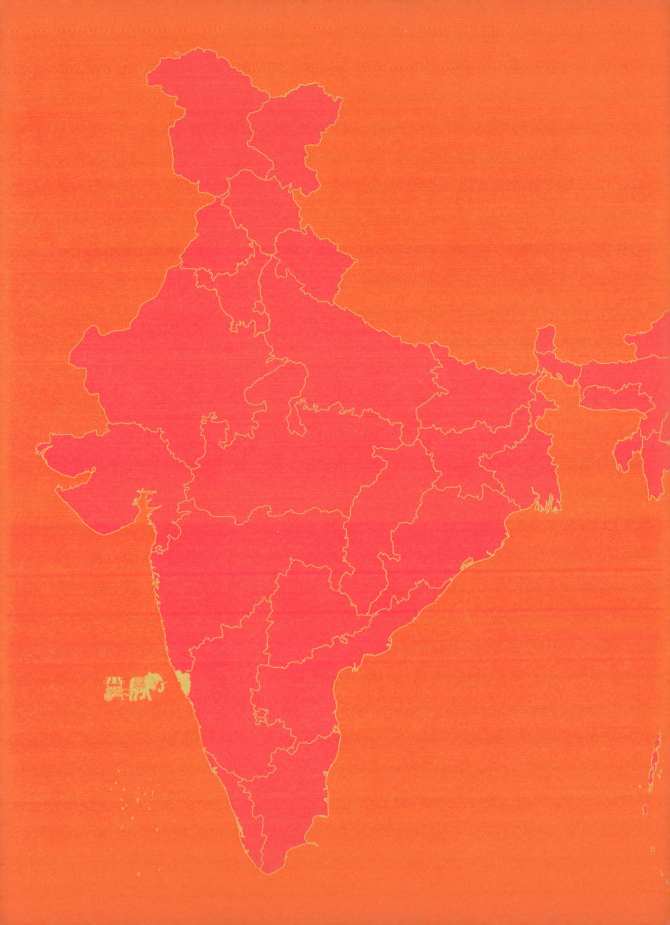

GOA

GOA

Goa is located along India's west coast on the shore of the Arabian Sea. Its cuisine is an interesting amalgam of Hindu cooking traditions fused with ingredients brought from Portugese Catholic colonizers (notably red chillies and vinegar). Goa was a Portugese colony for over 450 years and this had a profound influence on the food of the region, creating another unique Indian cuisine.

Seafood and coconut feature heavily in Goan cuisine, but most distinct of all is the use of kokum – a sour fruit that looks like a tomato – and vinegar. Sour flavours are preferred, and many dishes feature one noticeable and indispensable ingredient: toddy vinegar, which is made from the fermented sap of the stems of the coconut palm. It is frequently used for pickling and preserving fish, and is a key ingredient of the world-famous *Vindaloo* (see page 160). Tangy tamarind is another favourite souring agent.

Being coastal, it is no surprise that a Goan meal is considered incomplete if it does not feature fish or seafood in some way. Kingfish is a commonly eaten variety, but others include pomfret, shark, tuna, sardines and mackerel. Among the favourite shellfish are crabs, prawns/shrimp, lobster, squid and mussels. This chapter features many classic Goan fish dishes: *Ambotik* (a hot and sour fish curry – page 167), *Reacheado* (a stuffed fish fry with Portugese flavours – page 158) and Prawns *Balchão* (another Portugese-inspired dish, similar to a pickle – page 159). *Sorak*, a coconut curry (page 163), is a unique dish that you really should try.

XACUTI CHICKEN

This is a delicious chicken dish from Goa, made with freshly roasted spices. Usually, it is a curry with gravy, but I have tweaked the recipe slightly to turn it into a dry tikka-like preparation, using the same flavours. The locals eat this with *pav* (fluffy bread rolls), although I like it served with plain rice. Feel free to serve it however you prefer.

Serves 4

500g/1lb 2oz boneless chicken thighs
melted butter, for basting
fresh coriander/cilantro leaves, to garnish

FIRST MARINADE
2 tbsp Ginger-Garlic Paste (see page 17)
pinch of salt
1 tsp ground turmeric

XACUTI POWDER
200g/7oz fresh coconut, grated (desiccated/dried shredded coconut also works if you can't find fresh)
16 dried Kashmiri chillies, broken
4 tbsp coriander seeds
2 tsp cumin seeds
2 tsp fennel seeds
10cm/4in cinnamon stick, broken in half
2 tsp black peppercorns
8 cloves
4 star anise
2 tbsp poppy seeds

SECOND MARINADE
4 tbsp Greek yogurt
4 tbsp vegetable oil
4 green chillies, chopped
4 tsp tamarind paste
1 tsp ground nutmeg
1 tsp salt

Place the chicken in a bowl and add the first marinade ingredients. Coat well and leave to marinate for 15–20 minutes.

Heat a dry frying pan over a low heat and roast the grated coconut for the xacuti powder for 5–7 minutes until just brown. Remove and set aside.

In the same pan, dry-roast the whole spices for the xacuti powder, except the poppy seeds, for 2 minutes, or just until they smell aromatic. Add the poppy seeds and roast for a further minute, then leave to cool. Transfer the roasted spices to a spice grinder along with most of the roasted coconut (saving a little for garnish) and bliz to a fine powder. Set aside.

For the second marinade, take another mixing bowl and combine all the ingredients with the xacuti powder. Mix well to make a fine paste. Apply this marinade to the chicken pieces, cover and refrigerate for at least 2–3 hours before cooking.

Preheat the grill/broiler to high.

Skewer the chicken pieces and grill/broil for 8–10 minutes. Remove from the grill, turn and baste with the melted butter, then grill for a further 8–10 minutes until fully cooked. Serve hot, sprinkled with fresh coriander leaves and the reserved coconut, with chutneys and bread rolls or rice.

FISH CAFREAL

A Goan delicacy, cafreal fish is very popular across the globe. The dish is usually made with bream marinated in a green Goan spice paste, but some people use chicken as well. The paste is a delicious mix of fresh coriander/cilantro with aromatics and spices that really packs a punch.

Serves 6

6 bream fillets (or other firm white fish) (400–600g/ 14oz–1lb 5oz each), washed
vegetable oil, for basting

FIRST MARINADE
¼ tsp ground turmeric
1 tbsp lime juice
1 tbsp Ginger-Garlic Paste (see page 17)
salt, to taste

SECOND MARINADE
160g/5½oz fresh coriander/ cilantro leaves, washed, plus extra to serve
8–10 green chillies, washed
20g/¾oz fresh root ginger, washed
12 garlic cloves, peeled
2 tbsp malt vinegar or tamarind paste

CAFREAL SPICE MIX
1 tbsp poppy seeds
7–8 whole black peppercorns
5cm/2in cinnamon stick
4–6 cloves
1 tsp cumin seeds

TO SERVE
pinch of Chaat Masala (store-bought or see page 15)
red onion rings
lemon wedges

For the first marinade, place the fish fillets in a shallow bowl and sprinkle with a little salt, the turmeric and lime juice, then rub with the ginger-garlic paste and set aside for 15 minutes.

Meanwhile, in a food processor, blend all the ingredients for the second marinade to a smooth green paste.

Apply the second marinade to the fish pieces and rub it in well. Cover and refrigerate for at least 3 hours, but even better overnight.

For the cafreal spice mix, dry-roast all the spices in a frying pan over a low heat until fragrant, then blitz in a spice grinder to a fine powder.

When ready to cook the fish, preheat the oven to 200°C/ 180°C fan/400°F/Gas Mark 6.

Thread the marinated fish fillets onto metal skewers and place on a baking sheet. Bake in the oven for 8–10 minutes until almost done, then remove and baste the fish fillets with a little oil and return to the oven for another 2–3 minutes.

To serve, sprinkle the fish with chaat masala powder and serve with onion rings and lemon wedges and a sprinkling of fresh coriander leaves.

RECHEADO FISH FRY

This quick and easy recipe for stuffed fried fish is very popular in Goa. *Recheado* means 'stuffed' and the traditional *reacheado* masala is used not only for fish, but also for prawns/shrimp, other meat and vegetables. Here, we are not stuffing whole fish, but rather using the traditional masala paste to marinate fish fillets. The masala itself is bright red from the large number of red chillies, which makes it look fiery, but their heat is tempered by soaking in vinegar so it doesn't overpower.

Serves 4

4 fresh sea bass fillets (skin on) (see tip)
4 tbsp rapeseed/canola oil
lemon wedges, to serve

RECHEADO MASALA
100ml/3½fl oz/scant ½ cup coconut vinegar or white wine vinegar
8–10 Kashmiri red chillies, broken
1 small whole onion, roughly chopped
6–8 garlic cloves, peeled
2 tbsp chopped fresh root ginger
1 tsp whole peppercorns
1 tsp cumin seeds
4–5 cloves
2.5cm/1in cinnamon stick
½ tsp granulated sugar
½ tsp tamarind paste
pinch of salt

Combine all the ingredients for the masala in a bowl and set aside for 30 minutes. After this time, transfer the mixture to a food processor and blitz to a smooth paste.

Wash and dry the fish fillets thoroughly with paper towels, then place on a plate. Evenly apply the *recheado* masala to the fish pieces on both sides, then cover and set aside for 2–4 hours, or overnight in the refrigerator.

Heat the oil in a frying pan over a medium-high heat. When hot, pan-fry the fish fillets for about 3–4 minutes on each side until the flesh is opaque all the way through.

Serve hot with lemon wedges for squeezing.

TIP The fish should be firm and shiny. Press it with your finger – if it bounces back, the fish is fresh; if it leaves an impression, the fish is not fresh.

PRAWNS BALCHÃO

This fiery prawn/shrimp dish is a delicacy from Goan cuisine, and is similar to a pickle. *Balchão* is a method of cooking in a spicy and sour tomato-chilli sauce – it is also frequently used with fish or pork. This simple, quick recipe can be made in advance and kept refrigerated for a couple of days in an airtight container. Serve warm as a main course with rice. If you prefer, you can use fresh tiny shrimp and the resulting dish will be more like a side dish or chutney that can be served with poppadums. *Pictured on page 165.*

Serves 4

800g/1lb 12oz medium prawns/shrimp, cleaned and deveined
1 tbsp salt
500ml/17fl oz/2 cups rapeseed/canola oil
200g/7oz onions, finely chopped
4 tbsp chopped fresh root ginger
15 garlic cloves, chopped
100g/3½oz tomatoes, chopped
100g/3½oz/scant ½ cup granulated sugar
2 tbsp dried prawns/shrimp, roasted and ground to a powder in a pestle and mortar
170ml/6fl oz/¾ cup coconut vinegar or malt vinegar
4–6 green chillies, slit

FOR THE MASALA PASTE
15 dried Kashmiri chillies
1 tsp cumin seeds
2 tsp ground turmeric
1 tsp black peppercorns
100ml/3½fl oz/scant ½ cup malt vinegar

Mix the prawns with the salt and set aside for 20 minutes. This will draw out any excess water. Drain and pat dry.

To make the masala paste, roast the dried chillies, cumin seeds, turmeric and peppercorns in a dry pan until they start to release their aromas. Transfer to a food processor along with the vinegar and blitz to a fine paste.

Heat half of the oil in a deep pan over a medium-high heat. Add the prawns and fry for 3–4 minutes only. Remove with a slotted spoon to a plate and set aside.

Heat the remaining oil in a separate large pan over a medium heat. When hot, add the onions, ginger and garlic, and fry until golden. Add the masala paste and fry for 10–15 minutes over a low heat. Add the chopped tomatoes and cook until the tomato turns soft and pulpy. Add the fried prawns, sugar, dried powdered prawns and the vinegar. Stir, then add the slit green chillies and cook for 7–10 minutes.

Leave to cool, or serve warm.

PORK VINDALOO

Pork *vindaloo*, with its iconic vinegar tang, is a classic Goan dish and so popular worldwide that you will find it in almost every Indian restaurant. Even though *vindaloo* curry is well-known for its high level of heat, you can adjust it to taste, reducing the amount of red chillies used in the marinade for a milder dish.

Serves 4

700g/1lb 9oz pork leg, cut into bite-size pieces
5–6 tbsp rapeseed/canola oil
1 head of garlic, cloves cut into slivers
300g/10½oz onions, finely chopped
200g/7oz tomatoes, finely chopped (or use canned chopped tomatoes)
½ tsp chilli powder
1 tsp Kashmiri chilli powder
2 bay leaves
salt, to taste
2 tbsp chopped fresh coriander/cilantro, to garnish

MARINADE

3 dried red chillies
1 tbsp cumin seeds
1 tbsp coriander seeds
1 tsp seeds from black cardamom pods
1 tsp fenugreek seeds
5 cloves
2.5cm/1in cinnamon stick
10 black peppercorns
½ tsp ground turmeric
2 tbsp chopped green chillies
75ml/3fl oz/⅓ cup malt vinegar
1 tbsp soft brown sugar
2 tbsp Ginger-Garlic Paste (see page 17)

First, make the marinade. In a large, dry frying pan, roast all the dried whole spices, except the turmeric, over a medium heat until fragrant. Let cool slightly, then transfer to a spice grinder along with the turmeric and blitz to a fine powder.

In a food processor, combine the green chillies, vinegar, brown sugar and ginger-garlic paste, and blitz to a smooth paste. Add the spice powder and blitz to combine.

Put the pork in a large bowl, add the marinade and mix well. Leave to marinate for at least 2 hours, or ideally overnight – the longer the better.

When ready to cook, heat the oil in a large pan over a low heat. Add the garlic slivers and cook gently for about 10 minutes until soft and lightly brown (take care not to burn it). Use a slotted spoon to remove the garlic from the pan and set aside.

Heat the same oil over a medium-high heat until it is beginning to shimmer. Add the chopped onions with a pinch of salt and cook over a medium heat until soft and lightly golden. Increase the heat to high, stir in the chopped tomatoes, chilli powder, bay leaves and marinated pork, and cook for 5–6 minutes. Add just enough water to cover, then reduce the heat to very low and simmer for 1 hour, or until the pork is very tender, stirring from time to time. You may need to add more water if the pan starts to look dry.

Taste and adjust the salt or vinegar, if needed. Stir in the fried garlic and garnish with the chopped coriander. Serve with plain rice.

GOAN FISH CURRY

All seafood lovers enjoy this famous fish curry from Goa, as it is packed with flavour and just so easy to make. Tender pieces of thick white fish are cooked in a rich, aromatic, spiced tomato and coconut gravy. Garnish with sliced fresh green chillies for a bit of extra heat. It goes very well with plain rice or chapati.

Serves 4

SPICE PASTE
1 tbsp Kashmiri chilli powder
1 tbsp ground coriander
2 tsp ground cumin
1 tsp ground turmeric
½ tsp fenugreek powder
⅜ tsp ground cloves
6 garlic cloves, chopped
1 tbsp chopped fresh root ginger
2 tbsp tamarind purée
½ red onion, roughly chopped
6 tbsp water, or as needed

CURRY SAUCE
5 tbsp rapeseed/canola oil
½ tsp mustard seeds
150g/5oz onions, thinly sliced
1 tbsp tomato paste/tomato concentrate
75g/3oz canned chopped tomatoes
100ml/3½fl oz/scant ½ cup water
400ml/14fl oz/1⅔ cups coconut milk
1 tsp granulated sugar
1 tsp salt
¼ tsp chilli powder
1 fresh tomato, cut into 8 wedges
2 green chillies, halved and deseeded
800g/1lb 12oz thick white fish fillets (ideally belly cut), cut into 8 equal-sized pieces

TO GARNISH
2 tbsp chopped fresh coriander/cilantro
2 green chillies, finely sliced

Place all the spice paste ingredients in a food processor and blitz to a smooth paste. Add more water, if needed. Set aside.

Heat the oil for the curry sauce in a large pan over a medium heat. Add the mustard seeds and let them sizzle for 30 seconds (careful – they might pop!), then add the sliced onions and sauté until light golden in colour. Add the spice paste and cook for 6–8 minutes until most of the moisture has evaporated.

Increase the heat to high, add the tomato paste and canned tomatoes, and cook, stirring, for 5–6 minutes.

Add the measured water, coconut milk, sugar, salt and chilli powder, bring to a gentle simmer and reduce the heat to low. Add the tomato wedges and green chillies, and simmer for 4–5 minutes, stirring every now and then, until the sauce has thickened.

Stir in the fish pieces and cook for 3–4 minutes until the fish flakes easily, then remove from the heat and transfer to a serving bowl.

Garnish with coriander and fresh green chillies, and serve with rice.

SORAK

Sorak is a mildly spiced and tangy coconut-based curry, perfect with boiled or steamed rice, sautéed vegetables or pickles, and fried fish. It is normally made in the monsoon season. If you have a clay pot, do use it instead of a regular saucepan for an authentic flavour. *Pictured overleaf (left).*

Serves 4

60g/2oz fresh coconut, grated
8 dried Kashmiri chillies
8 garlic cloves
10 black peppercorns
½ tsp ground turmeric
¼ tsp cumin seeds
2 tbsp coriander seeds
1 tbsp tamarind paste
400ml/14fl oz/1⅔ cups water, or as needed
4 tbsp coconut oil
120g/4oz onions, finely chopped
2–4 green chillies
salt, to taste

Combine the grated coconut, dried chillies, garlic, peppercorns, turmeric, cumin seeds, coriander seeds and tamarind paste in a food processor and blitz to a smooth paste, adding up to 170ml/6fl oz/¾ cup of the water gradually as needed (you might not need it all).

Heat the coconut oil in a heavy pan or a clay pot over a medium heat. When hot, add the onions and sauté until translucent (do not brown them). Add the spice paste and sauté for 2–3 minutes.

If there is any remaining spice paste in the food processor, swill it out a few tablespoons of water and add it to the pot. Add the remaining water and mix well. Add the green chillies and salt, to taste. Bring to the boil, then reduce to a simmer and cook for a final 5 minutes, or until you reach your desired consistency.

Serve hot with steamed rice or *pao* (bread rolls).

AMBOTIK

Ambot means "sour" and *tik* means "hot and spicy" in Konkannim. In Goa, they make this hot and sour prawn/shrimp curry for festive occasions, but you can also enjoy it as a speciality in restaurants and beach shacks throughout the region.

Serves 4

10–12 jumbo prawns/shrimp, shelled and deveined
pinch of salt
8 garlic cloves, chopped
2 tbsp chopped fresh root ginger
½ tsp ground turmeric
1 tsp cumin seeds
1 tsp black peppercorns
1 tbsp tamarind purée
6 Kashmiri red chillies
100ml/3½fl oz/scant ½ cup rapeseed/canola oil
500g/1lb 2oz onions, sliced
2 tbsp canned chopped tomatoes, blitzed to a purée
1 tsp Kashmiri chilli powder
2 green chillies, slit
150ml/5fl oz/⅔ cup water

Sprinkle the prawns with salt and set aside for a few minutes.

Combine the garlic, ginger, turmeric, cumin seeds, peppercorns, tamarind purée and red chillies in a food processor and blitz to a smooth paste.

Heat the oil in a sauté pan over a medium heat. Add the onions and sauté until golden brown. Add the chopped tomato purée and Kashmiri chilli powder and cook for 5–6 minutes, then add the spice paste and green chillies, and cook until the oil starts to separate. Add the measured water and bring to the boil, then add the prawns and cook until tender, about 8–10 minutes.

Serve hot with rice or bread.

TIP If you prefer a less spicy or mild dish, you can always reduce the spice paste quantity and number of green chillies.

BEBINCA

Bebinca is a popular multilayered Goan cake, with a rich golden-brown colour and enticing flavours of coconut, vanilla and date syrup. An Indo-Portugese delicacy, it is a must at nearly all Goan religious and secular festivals, including Christmas and Easter. This version is slightly less sweet than is traditional, as I prefer it that way. At my restaurant, we serve it topped with a sprinkle of demerara sugar, blowtorched to an extra-crunchy sweet finish, but you can also finish it with a simple drizzle of date syrup, for extra sweetness.

Serves 6–8

240g/8oz/2 cups plain/all-purpose flour
large pinch of salt
600ml/20fl oz/2½ cups coconut milk
4 eggs
½ tsp ground nutmeg
2 tsp vanilla extract
2 tbsp date syrup, plus (optional) extra to serve
2 tbsp caster/superfine sugar
200ml/7fl oz/scant 1 cup melted ghee

Preheat the oven to 180°C/160°C fan/350°F/Gas 4 or preheat your grill/broiler to high.

In a mixing bowl, combine the flour, salt and coconut milk and whisk until there are no lumps. Add the eggs, nutmeg and vanilla extract and whisk until smooth.

Equally divide the batter between 2 bowls. To one bowl, add the date syrup and whisk to form a light brown batter. To the other bowl, add the sugar and whisk until the sugar is fully dissolved.

Brush a 30 x 15cm/12 x 6in baking dish with 2 teaspoons of the melted ghee. Pour in 2 ladlefuls of the white batter and bake in the oven or pop under the grill for 5 minutes until set.

Remove the dish from the oven, sprinkle over 2 more teaspoons of ghee and add 2 ladlefuls of the brown batter. Bake/grill for another 5 minutes, or until set.

Continue the above process, adding ghee and alternating batters, then baking/grilling, until all of the batters have been used up and/or the cake reaches the brim of the dish. Allow to cool for few minutes.

Turn the cake out of the dish, cut into small slices and serve warm, drizzled with extra date syrup, if wished, with a scoop of ice cream or sorbet on the side.

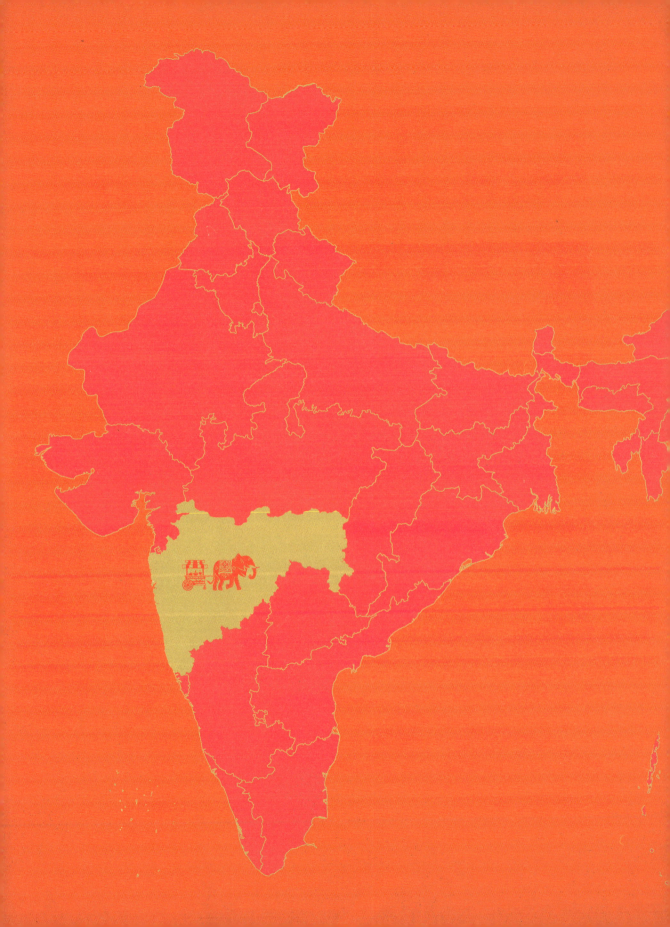

MAHARASHTRA

MAHARASHTRA

The region of Maharashtra on India's western peninsula covers an enormous geographical area. As a result, Maharashtrian (sometimes called Marathi) cuisine is well known for its diversity. Each local area in the region has its own subtle differences and food identity. From Kolhapuri to Malvani (Konkani), from Varhadhi to Khandeshi cuisines, every individual cuisine uses its own local spices and ingredients to create unique flavour combinations.

In the southern region of Malvan, the cuisine relies on seafood, whereas the majority of Maharashtrians, while not averse to eating meat, fish and eggs, are mostly lacto-vegetarian. Until recently, meat was traditionally used sparsely, or only by the well off. In terms of staples, those in the north or who live in urban areas prefer wheat-based roti or chapati, while those on the interior plateau and in coastal areas prefer dal and rice. In the capital, Mumbai, street foods such as *Vada Pav* (see page 176) and *Poha* (page 175) are popular. Meals are often served as a *thali* – small dishes arranged on a large platter with flatbreads and rice. Among other things, a *thali* usually features dal, a *bhaji* (vegetable dish), chutney and salad.

Classics I've chosen to feature include *Amti Dal* (page 185), a staple of the region; *Ghati Masala* Prawns (page 180); a dark, rich Mutton *Kala Masala* (page 179); *Malvani* (page 189), a spicy, coconut-heavy chicken curry; and *Paneer Kolhapuri* (page 186), a vegetarian dish for lovers of chilli heat. For those with a sweet tooth, *Aamras* (page 190) is a traditional pulped mango dessert served with deep-fried *pooris* – an indulgent treat.

POHA

Poha is a simple, light and quick breakfast or all-day snack dish made with flattened rice, peanuts and spices. Variations are found around India, sometimes adding seasonal greens, roasted peanuts, lime juice or *aloo bhujia* (spicy crisp-fried potato noodles – I really like to add some of these to boost the recipe when I have them – they can be bought in any Indian grocery store or supermarket). My mother always added a little bit of sugar too – she loved this served with a cup of masala tea.

Serves 4

250g/9oz/2¾ cups medium-grade *poha* (beaten rice flakes)
3 tbsp rapeseed/canola oil
6–8 tbsp peanuts or cashews
1½ tsp mustard seeds
1½ tsp cumin seeds
200g/7oz onions, finely chopped
pinch of asafoetida
2 sprigs of curry leaves
4 green chillies, slit or chopped
100g/3½oz tomatoes, chopped
150g/5oz potatoes, cut into 1cm/½in cubes (or ½ cup chopped mixed veggies) (optional)
1 tsp salt, or to taste
½ tsp ground turmeric (or more, for colour, if you like)
½ tsp hot chilli powder
1½ tsp Poha Magic Masala (see page 15)
juice of 2 lemons, or to taste
4 tbsp chopped fresh coriander/cilantro
plain yogurt, to serve

Place the *poha* flakes in a colander or strainer and rinse under cold running water, then drain thoroughly. Repeat this process twice more, then spread over a wide plate in a single layer and set aside.

Heat the oil in a deep pan (that has a lid) over a medium heat. When hot, add the nuts and fry until golden and crunchy. Remove with a slotted spoon to a plate and set aside.

To the same pan, add the mustard and cumin seeds. When they begin to pop, add the chopped onions, asafoetida, curry leaves and green chillies. Sauté until the onions are lightly golden brown.

Add the tomatoes. If using, add the cubed potatoes or mixed veggies at this point and sauté for 1 minute. Cover and cook over a low heat until soft and cooked through. If the pan starts to look a little dry, add a splash of water.

Add the *poha* along with the salt, turmeric and chilli powder, mix well, then cover and cook over a very low heat until the *poha* starts to steam. If you feel the pan is too dry, sprinkle in some water and continue to steam the poha. Remove from the heat when the *poha* has softened and is piping hot.

Sprinkle in the poha magic masala and mix well, then check the seasoning and squeeze over some lemon juice, to taste. Serve, garnished with the fresh coriander and roasted nuts, with some plain yogurt on the side.

VADA PAV

Vada pav is a popular and delicious Maharashtrian street food of fried batter-coated mashed potato dumplings sandwiched in a *pav* (soft bread roll), which is also loaded with sweet tamarind and green chutneys. I recommend adding some Ghati Masala (see page 13) and fried green chillies too, for a unique flavour.

Serves 8

rapeseed/canola oil, for deep-frying
8 *pav* or soft dinner rolls
3–4 fried green chillies sprinkled with salt (optional)

GREEN CHUTNEY

30g/1oz/1 cup chopped fresh coriander/cilantro
1–2 garlic cloves, chopped
squeeze of lemon juice
2–3 green chillies, chopped
pinch of salt

SWEET TAMARIND CHUTNEY (OR USE STORE-BOUGHT)

100g/3½oz seedless tamarind pulp
250ml/9fl oz/1 cup hot water, or as needed
1 tsp vegetable oil
½ tsp cumin seeds
½ tsp ground ginger
¼ tsp red chilli powder
1 tbsp ground coriander
pinch of asafoetida
2 tbsp granulated sugar
5 tbsp powdered jaggery, or to taste
pinch of salt or black salt

POTATO STUFFING

350g/12oz potatoes
6–7 garlic cloves, peeled
1–2 green chillies
3 tbsp rapeseed/canola oil
½ tsp mustard seeds
7–8 curry leaves
pinch of asafoetida
⅛ tsp ground turmeric
2 tbsp chopped fresh coriander/cilantro
pinch of salt

BATTER

150g/5oz/generous 1⅓ cups gram flour/besan
pinch of asafoetida
½ tsp ground turmeric
pinch of bicarbonate of soda/baking soda (optional)
pinch of salt

First, make the chutneys for serving.

In a food processor, blitz together all the green chutney ingredients with a splash of water until smooth. Avoid making a watery chutney.

For the sweet tamarind chutney, soak the tamarind in enough hot water to cover for 30–40 minutes. With your hands, squeeze the pulp from the tamarind in the same bowl or pan. Strain the pulp and keep aside.

CONTINUES OVERLEAF

Heat the oil in a small pan over a medium heat, then reduce the heat to low, add the cumin seeds and let them crackle. Add the ground ginger, chilli powder, ground coriander and asafoetida, stir well and then add the strained tamarind pulp. Cook for 4–5 minutes. Add the sugar, jaggery and salt and cook for a final 10–15 minutes until you have a thick mixture. Leave to cool.

For the potato stuffing, boil, drain and mash the potatoes, then set aside.

In a pestle and mortar, crush the garlic and green chillies to a semi-fine paste.

Heat the oil in a small pan over a medium heat. When hot, add the mustard seeds, then when they crackle, add the curry leaves and asafoetida. Sauté for about 15 seconds. Add the garlic and green chilli paste along with the turmeric and sauté until the raw aroma of garlic goes away. Pour the mixture into the mashed potatoes, add the chopped coriander and salt, and mix well.

Form the mashed potato mixture into 8 small–medium balls and flatten slightly into patties. Cover and set aside.

In a medium bowl, combine the batter ingredients, using just enough water to make a smooth and thick yet flowing batter. If the batter becomes too thin, add 1 or 2 tablespoons more flour; if too thick, add a little more water. Set aside.

Heat enough oil for deep-frying in a large, deep pan to 180°C/350°F. Dip the potato patties into the batter and coat evenly, then gently lower into the hot oil (you may need to cook in batches). Fry until one side becomes crisp and lightly golden, then gently turn with a slotted spoon to fry the other side. Keep turning a couple of times until the *vadas* are evenly golden on all sides. Remove to drain on paper towels.

Serve while still hot or warm. Slice the *pav* (bread rolls) in half, not quite all the way through. Spread the green chutney on one half of the rolls and the sweet tamarind chutney on the other halves, then sandwich the *vadas* in between. Serve immediately, or else the *pav* becomes soggy, with some fried salted green chillies, if using, on the side.

TIP The sweet tamarind chutney can be stored in an airtight jar in the refrigerator for 4–6 weeks. Serve with *chaat* or snacks.

MUTTON KALA MASALA

Mutton *kala masala* is inspired by Maharashtrian *goda* (or *kala*) *masala*. This is a famous spice mix made of charred whole spices, which is what gives it its dark brown, almost black colour. I few years ago I made a whole chicken dish with *kala masala* that was a super hit with my restaurant guests. This mutton version is very traditional.

Serves 4

100ml/3½fl oz/scant ½ cup rapeseed/canola oil
5–6 cloves
10 black peppercorns
1–2 bay leaves
1 tsp cumin seeds
1 cinnamon stick
2–3 green cardamom pods
2 black cardamom pods
2 dried Kashmiri chillies
300g/10½oz onions, thinly sliced
3–4 tsp Ginger-Garlic Paste (see page 17)
2 tsp *degi mirch* powder
2–3 tsp Kala Masala (see page 14)
100g/3½oz tomatoes, thinly sliced
800g/1lb 12oz mutton, cut into bite-size chunks
7–8 garlic cloves, crushed
2–3 green chillies, slit
400ml/14fl oz/1⅔ cups water
salt, to taste
2 tbsp chopped fresh coriander/cilantro, to garnish

Heat the oil in a large, heavy pan (that has a tight-fitting lid) over a medium heat. When hot, add all the whole dried spices and stir for a minute or so, then add the onions along with a pinch of salt and fry until golden brown. Add the ginger-garlic paste and fry until the raw aroma is gone, then add the *degi mirch* and kala masala and mix well. Add a splash of water so that the spices don't burn, then add the sliced tomatoes and mix well. Cover and cook over a low heat, stirring occasionally, until the tomatoes have disintegrated and the oil starts to separate.

Remove the lid and add the mutton pieces, crushed garlic and green chillies, and simmer for about 10 minutes over a high heat. Add the measured water and stir well, then taste and adjust the seasoning. Cover and cook over a low heat for 25–30 minutes, or until the meat is cooked.

Serve hot, garnished with the fresh coriander.

MAHARASHTRA

GHATI MASALA PRAWNS

These crispy batter-fried prawns/shrimp are one of the signature dishes in my restaurants and very popular. This recipe is made by those who live in the small villages, or ghats, around Maharashtra. *Ghati masala* is a hot spice mix used in many of their snacks and curries. I have slightly tweaked the recipe to tone down the heat a little to work well with prawns. This is so easy to make – I know you'll love it. *Pictured overleaf (left).*

Serves 4

40 small peeled prawns/shrimp
2 sprigs of curry leaves, finely chopped
2 tsp Kashmiri chilli powder
juice of 1 lime, plus wedges to serve
3 tbsp rice flour
3 tbsp cornflour/cornstarch
pinch of salt
1½ tsp Ginger-Garlic Paste (see page 17)
2 green chillies, deseeded and chopped
rapeseed/canola oil, for deep-frying
2 tsp Ghati Masala (store-bought or see page 13)
1 tbsp grated fresh coconut
2 tbsp chopped fresh coriander/cilantro

Place the prawns in a bowl and toss with the chopped curry leaves, 1 teaspoon of the chilli powder and a dash of lime juice. Set aside to marinate while you prepare the rest of the ingredients.

In a separate bowl, combine the rice flour and cornflour, salt, remaining teaspoon of chilli powder, the ginger-garlic paste and chopped green chillies. Add just enough water to form a thick batter.

Heat enough oil for deep-frying in a deep pan or deep-fat fryer to 170°C/340°F.

Coat the prawns in the batter, ensuring they are well covered. Deep-fry for about 4 minutes until golden (you may need to cook in batches), then remove with a slotted spoon to drain on paper towels.

Serve hot, sprinkled with the ghati masala, fresh coconut and chopped coriander, with lime wedges on the side for squeezing over.

BHARLI VANGI

In this vegetarian Maharashtrian delicacy, baby aubergines/eggplants are stuffed with a spicy stuffing and slow-cooked in an onion gravy until tender. The dish can be prepared dry or with extra gravy, as you prefer, and served with roti or chapati. *Pictured overleaf (right).*

Serves 4

8 baby aubergines/eggplants
1 tsp salt, or to taste, plus extra to sprinkle inside the aubergines
4 tbsp rapeseed/canola oil
1 tsp mustard seeds
1 tsp cumin seeds
8 curry leaves
4 green chillies, slit
1 onion, finely chopped
100ml/3½fl oz/scant ½ cup water
2 tbsp chopped fresh coriander/cilantro, to garnish

STUFFING

100g/3½oz roasted peanuts (skinless)
4 garlic cloves
2.5cm/1in piece of fresh root ginger
1 tbsp jaggery
1 tbsp Garam Masala (store-bought or see page 12)
1 tsp hot chilli powder
½ tsp ground turmeric

Slit the aubergines vertically into 4 quarters, running the knife from top to bottom but without cutting through the stem ends. Sprinkle some salt inside the slits and set aside for about 10 minutes.

In a food processor, blitz together all the stuffing ingredients with a splash of water. The stuffing should be thick and wet.

Heat the oil in a sauté pan (that has a lid) over a medium heat. When hot, add the mustard seeds, cumin seeds, curry leaves and slit green chillies. Once the seeds crackle, add the chopped onion and teaspoon of salt, and sauté until nicely browned.

Stuff each aubergine with the stuffing mixture – about 2 tablespoons per aubergine should be about right. Gently place the stuffed aubergines over the onion gravy. Add the measured water, cover and cook over a low heat for about 15 minutes, then gently turn the aubergines over and cook on the other side for a further 15 minutes. If the sauce starts to look too dry, add more water, as needed.

Serve hot, garnished with fresh coriander.

DAL CHICKEN

Chicken cooked with red lentils is one of the easiest staple curries in Maharashtrian cuisine. With limited ingredients it nevertheless strikes the perfect balance between nutritious and delicious.

Serves 4

100g/3½oz/generous ⅓ cup split red lentils
100ml/3½fl oz/scant ½ cup rapeseed/canola oil
1 bay leaf
1 cinnamon stick
2 black cardamom pods
6–8 black peppercorns
250g/9oz onions, finely chopped
100g/3½oz tomatoes, chopped
1 green chilli, chopped
1 tsp finely chopped fresh root ginger
¼ tsp ground turmeric
1 tsp salt, or to taste
700ml/24fl oz/3 cups water
750g/1lb 10oz chicken thighs (boneless or on-the-bone)
1 tbsp Kala Masala (see page 14)
2 tbsp lemon juice
4 tbsp chopped fresh coriander/cilantro, to garnish

TEMPERING

1 tbsp rapeseed/canola oil
1 tsp cumin seeds
1 dried red chilli
3 garlic cloves, finely chopped
½ tsp hot chilli powder

Wash the lentils under cold running water several times, then place in a bowl with fresh water and leave to soak for 20–30 minutes. Drain.

Heat the oil in a large, deep pan (that has a lid) over a medium heat. When hot, add the whole spices and let crackle, then add the chopped onions and sauté until golden brown. Add the soaked lentils, tomatoes, green chilli, ginger, turmeric, salt and measured water. Bring to the boil, then reduce the heat to low, cover and simmer for 15–20 minutes.

Stir the chicken pieces into the pan along with the kala masala. Cover again and simmer for a further 20–25 minutes, or until the chicken is tender and cooked through.

For the tempering, heat the oil in a small pan over a medium heat. Add the cumin seeds, then when they start to sizzle add the dried red chilli and chopped garlic. Fry until the garlic is brown, then add the chilli powder. Pour the tempering straight into the dal chicken along with the lemon juice. Mix gently, check the seasoning and cook over a low heat for a final 5 minutes.

Serve hot, garnished with fresh coriander, with plain boiled rice or chapati.

AMTI DAL

This Maharashtrian *amti dal* recipe is very much everyday comfort food in India and every single community has their own version of this classic. Easy to cook, the combination of sweet, tangy and spicy flavours are as ideal served with plain rice as they are eaten alone.

Serves 4

1 tbsp ghee
1 tsp mustard seeds
½ tsp cumin seeds
pinch of asafoetida
10–12 curry leaves
2 dried red chillies
1 green chilli, finely chopped
½ tsp ground turmeric
120ml/4fl oz/½ cup water
1 tbsp Kala Masala (see page 14)
¼ tsp Kashmiri chilli powder
1½ tsp jaggery
2 tbsp tamarind paste
2 tbsp grated fresh coconut
1 tsp salt
2 tbsp finely chopped fresh coriander/cilantro

LENTILS
350g/12oz/2 cups toor dal (yellow lentils)
600ml/20fl oz/2½ cups water
1 tsp salt
½ tsp ground turmeric

Wash the lentils under cold running water several times, then place in a bowl with fresh water and leave to soak for 20–30 minutes. Drain.

In a saucepan, combine the measured water with the salt and ground turmeric. Add the drained lentils, then bring to the boil. Simmer over a medium heat for about 15–20 minutes, or until the lentils are soft.

In a large pan, heat the ghee over a medium heat. When hot, add the mustard and cumin seeds, asafoetida, curry leaves and dried red chillies, and briefly sauté until the seeds start to crackle. Reduce the heat to low, add the green chilli and turmeric, and sauté for a minute, then add the cooked toor dal and the measured water. Mix well, then add the kala masala, chilli powder, jaggery, tamarind, coconut and salt. Mix again, bring to the boil, then simmer for 8–10 minutes over a medium heat until it reaches your preferred consistency.

Serve, garnished with the fresh coriander, with steamed rice on the side.

PANEER KOLHAPURI

This is a hot vegetarian dish from Maharashtra, specifically from the Kolhapur region. Kolhapuri cuisine is a bit on the spicier side – they use lot of whole red chillies, coconut and dry-roasted whole spices to blend into a versatile masala paste. The same base could be used to make a vegetable or chicken curry that will feel authentically Maharashtrian.

Serves 4

100ml/3½fl oz/scant ½ cup rapeseed/canola oil
50g/1¾oz cashews
200g/7oz tomatoes, roughly chopped
300g/10½oz onions, finely chopped
1 tbsp Ginger-Garlic Paste (see page 17)
½ tsp ground turmeric
1½ tsp hot chilli powder
½ tsp Kashmiri chilli powder
1 tbsp salt, or to taste
1 tbsp Kolhapuri Masala (see page 16)
500g/1lb 2oz paneer, cut into 2.5cm/1in cubes
2 tbsp finely chopped fresh coriander/cilantro, plus extra to garnish

Heat 1 tablespoon of the oil in a sauté pan over a medium heat. When hot, add the cashews and sauté for 4–5 minutes until golden. Remove with a slotted spoon to drain on paper towels and let cool.

Transfer the cooled nuts to a food processor along with the tomatoes and blitz to a purée.

Add the remaining oil to the sauté pan and reheat over a medium heat. When hot, add the onions and sauté until golden brown. Add the ginger-garlic paste and sauté for a few seconds until the raw aroma goes away. Add the turmeric, chilli powders and salt, and mix well. Stir in the cashew-tomato purée along with the kolhapuri masala and continue to cook over a medium heat until the oil starts to separate. Taste for seasoning and adjust to your preference.

Add the paneer cubes and chopped coriander and cook for a minute or two to warm through, gently mixing with a spatula.

Serve hot, garnished with fresh coriander, with garlic naan or chapatis.

MALVANI CHICKEN CURRY

This is a spicy and flavourful chicken dish from the coastal region of Maharashtra, Malvan. An authentic Malvani chicken curry is made with a hot and aromatic masala and lots of coconut. This is a perfect chicken curry for all the spice lovers out there.

Serves 4–6

1.5kg/3lb 5oz whole chicken, cut into pieces
1½ tbsp Ginger-Garlic Paste (see page 17)
½ tsp ground turmeric
1 tsp salt, or to taste
3 tbsp rapeseed/canola oil
2–3 bay leaves
1 large onion, chopped
3–4 large garlic cloves, crushed
700ml/24fl oz/3 cups water
handful of fresh coriander/cilantro leaves, to garnish

MALVANI MASALA

8–10 dried red chillies
1 tbsp coriander seeds
½ tsp cumin seeds
½ tsp caraway seeds
½ tsp mustard seeds
½ tsp sesame seeds
2 blades of mace
¼ tsp ground nutmeg
1 star anise
1 tsp fennel seeds
4–5 cloves
2.5cm/1in cinnamon stick
3–4 green cardamom pods
1 black cardamom pod
10 black peppercorns
25g/1oz/1¼ cups desiccated/dried shredded coconut
pinch of asafoetida

ONION-COCONUT PASTE

1 tbsp vegetable oil
2 large onions, sliced
5–6 garlic cloves, peeled
100g/3½oz/1½ cups grated fresh coconut

Marinate the chicken in the ginger-garlic paste, ground turmeric and salt, and set aside.

Dry-roast all the masala ingredients in a dry frying pan until you get a nice nutty aroma. Let cool for a few minutes, then grind to a fine powder.

For the onion-coconut paste, heat the oil in a large, heavy pan over a medium heat. When hot, add the sliced onions and garlic, and sauté for 2–3 minutes until soft. Stir in the freshly grated coconut and cook for 10–12 minutes until golden brown, then remove from the heat and let cool for some time before grinding it into a paste with a splash of water.

Add the 3 tablespoons of oil to the same pan and heat it over a medium heat. When hot, add the bay leaves and chopped onion, and sauté for 2–3 minutes until golden brown. Add the garlic and the marinated chicken and fry for 5 minutes until the chicken is browned on all sides. Stir in the masala powder, then add the onion-coconut paste and cook for 5–6 minutes. Add the measured water, cover and cook, stirring from time to time, for a further 18–20 minutes until the chicken is cooked through and the oil starts to separate. Check the seasoning and add more salt if required.

Serve hot, garnished with the fresh coriander, with chapatis on the side.

TIP If you prefer a milder dish, you can halve the number of dried red chillies.

AAMRAS WITH SAFFRON POORIS

Aamras is a mango delicacy that is popular in both Maharashtra and Gujarat – a summer delight in a bowl. So simple to make, I often prepare it on weekends during the hot Indian summer. It makes a delicious after-dinner dessert with hot saffron *pooris*, although I can eat it at just about any time.

Serves 4

AAMRAS
400g/14oz fresh ripe alphonso mangoes, peeled and flesh chopped (prepared weight) (or use store-bought mango pulp)
½ tsp ground cardamom
¼ tsp ground ginger
pinch of saffron strands
granulated sugar, to taste
water or milk, as required
1 tbsp chopped cashews or pistachios

SAFFRON POORIS
200g/7oz/1¾ cups medium chapati flour (*atta*)
2 tbsp fine semolina
¼ tsp carom seeds/ajwain
pinch of salt
a few saffron strands disssolved in a little warm milk
1 tbsp rapeseed/canola oil, plus extra for greasing and deep-frying
100ml/3½fl oz/scant ½ cup water

First, make the *aamras*. In a blender, blitz the mango flesh together with the cardamom, ginger and saffron. Taste and add sugar, if required (this may depend on how sweet the mangoes are). To thin down the *aamras*, you can add some water or milk, if needed.

Divide the *aamras* among 4 small bowls and decorate with the chopped nuts. Chill in the refrigerator until ready to serve.

Start to make the saffron *pooris* about an hour before you are ready to serve. Combine the flour, semolina, carom seeds and salt in a large bowl. Add the saffron milk and mix well. Add the oil, then start to add the measured water, a little at a time, mixing at first and then kneading as the dough starts to come together. Knead the dough thoroughly, adding more water as needed, until you have a soft dough. The dough may be hard at first, and then sticky, but as you continue to knead it will soften. The dough should not be too soft but still a little stiff and tight. Cover and leave to rest for 30 minutes.

After 30 minutes, lightly knead the dough again, then divide into 16 balls of equal size. Cover and set aside for 10–15 minutes.

Heat enough oil for deep-frying in a large wok or deep pan to about 180°C/350°F.

Take a dough ball and slightly flatten it with your palms. Apply a little oil to it on both sides, then gently roll out with a rolling pin to about 6–8cm/2¼–3in in diameter.

Add one *poori* at a time to the hot oil and fry until both sides are crisp and golden, and the *poori* has puffed up. Remove with a slotted spoon to drain on paper towels. Continue to roll and cook the other *pooris* in the same way.

Serve the chilled *aamras* with 4 hot, crispy saffron *pooris* on the side of each bowl.

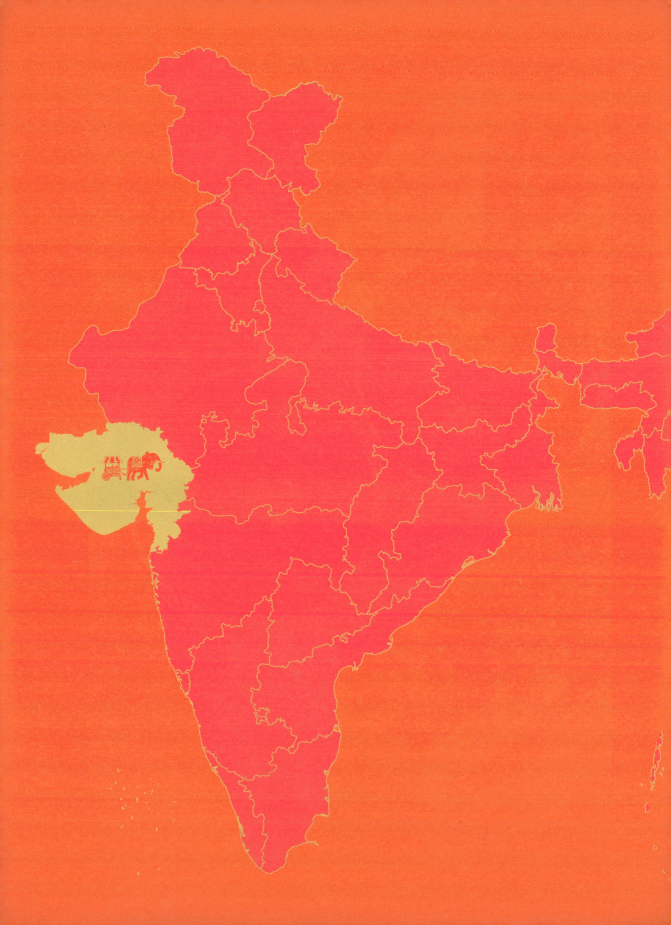

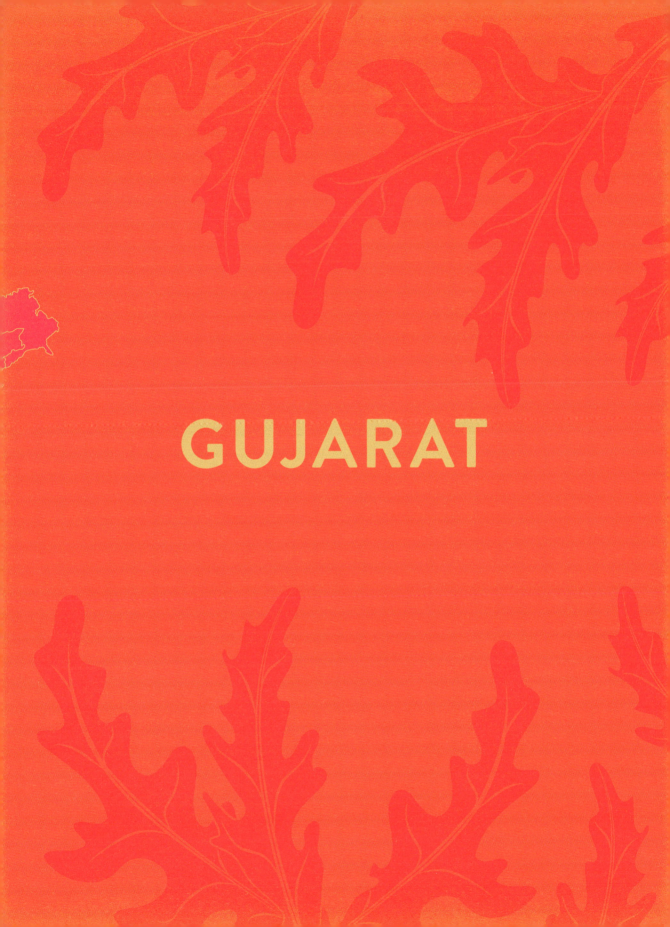

GUJARAT

GUJARAT

Gujarat, on the western coast of India, is a primarily vegetarian state, although some communities do still include seafood, chicken, eggs and mutton in their diets. This might seem surprising given their easy access to plentiful seafood along the coast, but the hot, dry climate, agrarian nature of their farming, and predominance of the Vaishnava sect of the Hindu religion means that vegetarianism became ingrained in the culture.

A typical Gujarati *thali* consists of roti, dal or curry, rice and *shaak* (a dish made up of several different combinations of vegetables and spices, which may be either spicy or sweet). The use of sugar or jaggery in meals is widespread and you will find that many Gujarati dishes are distinctively sweet, salty and spicy all at once, though with differing levels of heat.

Staples include *Khichdi* (rice and lentils, see page 199), *Kadhi* (a unique buttermilk-based soup, page 200) and *Dal Dhokli* (wholewheat dumplings in a thin dal, page 207). A cooling tomato *sabzi* (*Sev Tamater*, page 209) makes a great side dish to help offset dehydration in the fierce heat of the Gujarati summer. I have also included a couple of *shaak* curries in this chapter (pages 202 and 206) to represent a few non-vegetarian favourites of the region. And I couldn't leave out the classic *Dhokla* (page 210), a steamed savoury sponge cake tempered with curry leaves and spices, which I serve garnished in a modern way with a little salad of pea shoots, fresh coconut and baby beetroot.

GUJARAT

195

KHANDVI

This is a typical savoury snack food from Gujarat. Melt in the mouth and very moreish, these gram flour rolls are a delicious, healthy option for whenever hunger strikes. Spicy, sour and gently sweetened by the fresh coconut filling, they go well with a cup of chai.

Makes 12–14 / Serves 4

1cm/½in piece of fresh root ginger, peeled and chopped
1 green chilli, deseeded and chopped
150g/5oz/scant ⅔ cup plain yogurt
400ml/14fl oz/1⅔ cups water
½ tsp ground turmeric
pinch of asafoetida
1½ tsp salt
100g/3½oz/scant 1 cup gram flour/besan
1 tbsp rapeseed/canola oil, for greasing

FILLING

2 tbsp grated fresh coconut, plus extra to garnish
2 tbsp chopped fresh coriander/cilantro, plus extra to garnish

TEMPERING

1 tbsp rapeseed/canola oil
1 tsp mustard seeds
8–10 curry leaves
1 green chilli, chopped
2 tsp white sesame seeds

Grind the ginger and green chilli together in a pestle and mortar until you have a paste. Set aside.

Put the yogurt in a bowl, then add the water and stir until smoothly combined. Stir in the ginger-chilli paste, turmeric, asafoetida and salt. Now add the gram flour, whisking until all the lumps have dissolved and you have a smooth batter.

In a small bowl, mix together the filling ingredients. Set aside.

Pour the batter into a wide, deep pan and set over a very low heat. Stir constantly with a whisk while the batter heats up. The batter will slowly begin to thicken – keep on whisking. When the batter is very thick and coming away from the sides of the pan, it is ready to test – this can take 20–25 minutes.

Grease your work surface with a little oil. Use a palette knife to thinly spread a few teaspoons of batter onto the surface. Let it cool a little, then try to roll it up. If it will not roll, the batter needs to be cooked for longer. If the batter becomes too thick, it will be difficult to spread in a thin layer, so test frequently. When you are happy with the consistency, quickly pour the batter over the greased surface and swiftly spread it out thinly and evenly with a palette knife. Leave to cool.

Sprinkle the filling mixture sparingly over the cooled batter. Use a sharp knife to slice the batter into 8-cm/3-in strips. Gently roll each strip up into a roll and place on a serving plate. You may want to cut the strips in half to make smaller rolls. Arrange the rolls neatly next to each other.

In a small pan, heat the oil for tempering. When hot, add the mustard seeds and let crackle, then add the curry leaves and green chilli, and fry for a few seconds. Add the sesame seeds. As soon as they darken and start to crackle, pour the hot tempering mixture evenly over the rolls. Garnish with extra coconut and fresh coriander, and serve with Mint and Coriander Chutney (see page 18) on the side.

KHICHDI

Gujarati *khichdi* is my all-time favourite comfort food. I make it every week as it is light, good for digestion and a healthy quick-fix meal. There are so many variations of *khichdi* – each state and even family will have their own preferred style, but this one is particular to Gujarat. It can be made either with a medley of vegetables or without any vegetables at all, if you prefer.

Serves 4

100g/3½oz/½ cup basmati rice
160g/5½oz/scant 1 cup toor dal (split yellow pigeon peas)
3 tbsp rapeseed/canola oil
1 tsp mustard seeds
1 tsp cumin seeds
½ tsp black peppercorns
2.5cm/1in cinnamon stick
3–4 cloves
2 dried red chillies
pinch of asafoetida
8–10 curry leaves
1 onion, sliced
100g/3½oz aubergine/eggplant, cut into 2cm/¾in cubes
100g/3½oz potatoes, cut into 2cm/¾in cubes
50g/1¾oz green peas
2 tsp ginger paste
2 tsp garlic paste
100g/3½oz tomatoes, chopped
½ tsp ground turmeric
½ tsp hot chilli powder
500ml/17fl oz/2 cups hot water
2 tbsp ghee
salt, to taste

Wash the rice and lentils together, then leave to soak in plenty of water for 30 minutes. Drain and set aside.

Heat the oil in a large pan over a medium heat, then add the mustard seeds, cumin seeds, peppercorns, cinnamon, cloves and dried red chillies. When they start to crackle, add the asafoetida, curry leaves and sliced onion, and sauté until the onions are light brown. Add the aubergine/eggplant, potatoes, peas, ginger and garlic pastes, and sauté for 1–2 minutes over a low heat. Add the soaked rice and lentils along with the chopped tomatoes and sauté for a minute. Stir in the turmeric, chilli powder and salt, to taste, then add the measured hot water and the ghee. Cover and cook over a low heat for about 20–25 minutes until the rice and lentils are quite mushy and soft (in this dish, the rice and lentils are slightly overcooked for a smoother texture).

Serve hot with poppadums and pickles.

KADHI

Kadhi is a very popular dish across India and an essential part of Gujarati cuisine. Traditionally made from buttermilk or yogurt and gram flour/besan, it often features pakoras, but this easy version omits them. It makes for a quick, comforting lunch or dinner paired with a side of steamed basmati rice or chapati.

Serves 4

375g/13oz/1½ cups plain yogurt
2 tbsp gram flour/besan
1½ tsp ginger paste
3 green chillies, finely chopped
½ tsp ground turmeric
2 tsp sugar
2 tsp salt
700ml/24fl oz/3 cups water
1 tbsp fresh coriander/cilantro leaves, to garnish

TEMPERING

2 tsp ghee (or vegetable oil)
½ tsp mustard seeds
½ tsp cumin seeds
2 dried red chillies
2.5cm/1in cinnamon stick
4 cloves
8–10 curry leaves
pinch of asafoetida

In a large saucepan, combine the yogurt with the gram flour, ginger paste, green chillies, turmeric, sugar and salt. Whisk well so there are no lumps. You can use a hand blender for this too. Add the measured water and mix thoroughly until you have a lump-free, thin batter.

Set the pan over a medium heat and bring to the boil, while stirring continuously. You must stir constantly to avoid curdling and separating the yogurt. Reduce to a simmer while you prepare the tempering.

Heat the ghee or oil in a small pan over a medium-low heat. When hot, add the mustard and cumin seeds. When they crackle, add the dried chillies, cinnamon stick and cloves. After a few seconds, you will get a nice fragrance from the whole spices. Add the curry leaves and asafoetida, then pour the tempering into the yogurt pan. Stir well. Simmer for a further 5 minutes until the raw taste and aroma of gram flour goes away.

Remove from the heat, stir in the chopped coriander and serve.

GUJARAT

MURGHANU SHAAK

This is a home-style chicken curry cooked with potatoes, unique to Gujarat. The majority of people in Gujarat are vegetarian, but a few do eat non-vegetarian dishes as well, enjoying simple fare such as this. It is a delicious, quick-to-make recipe.

Serves 4

1 tbsp chopped fresh root ginger
1 tbsp chopped garlic
3 green chillies
1kg/2lb 4oz skinless, boneless chicken thighs, cut into bite-size pieces
100g/3½oz/generous ⅓ cup plain yogurt
2 tsp salt
100ml/3½fl oz/scant ½ cup rapeseed/canola oil
6 cloves
2 cinnamon sticks
2 star anise
2 green cardamom pods
2 black cardamom pods
15–20 fresh curry leaves
250g/9oz onions, chopped
2 tsp ground turmeric
100g/3½oz tomato purée/paste
200g/7oz potatoes, peeled and halved
2 tbsp chopped fresh coriander/cilantro
150ml/5fl oz/⅔ cup water
1 tbsp Garam Masala (store-bought or see page 12)

In a food processor, blitz together the ginger, garlic and green chillies until you have a paste.

Place the chicken pieces in a large bowl, add the yogurt, salt and ginger-garlic-chilli paste, mix well and set aside to marinate for at least 20–30 minutes.

Heat the oil in a large pan (that has a lid) over a medium heat. Add the whole spices and sauté for about 30 seconds. When they start crackling, add the onions and sauté until golden brown. Add the marinated chicken, turmeric and tomato purée, and stir well. Cover and cook for 10 minutes, or until the juices run from the chicken.

Add the potatoes, fresh coriander and measured water, cover and cook for a final 20–25 minutes, or until the chicken and potatoes are tender. Stir in the garam masala and remove from the heat.

Serve with rice or chapati and chutney.

THEPLA

Thepla is a flatbread made with wholemeal/wholewheat and millet flours, spices and herbs. Sometimes fenugreek leaves are also added to boost the flavour and nutrition profile. Thepla is a staple in Gujarati households and is eaten with mango pickle or with plain yogurt. Pictured overleaf (left).

Makes 8–9

80g/3oz fresh fenugreek leaves or 1 tbsp dried (optional)
180g/6¼oz/1¼ cups wholemeal/wholewheat flour, plus extra for dusting
50g/1¾oz/⅓ cup millet flour
3–4 tbsp gram flour/besan
1 tsp Ginger-Garlic paste (see page 17)
1–2 green chillies, finely chopped
½ tsp salt, or to taste
½ tsp hot chilli powder
½ tsp Garam Masala (store-bought or see page 12)
½ tsp ground turmeric
3 tbsp rapeseed/canola oil

If using fresh leaves, rinse the fenugreek in plenty of water and drain well. Chop finely and place in a mixing bowl. Add all the remaining ingredients, except the oil, to the bowl and begin to mix and then knead well. Sprinkle only enough water into the bowl as needed (some moisture will come from the fresh fenugreek leaves, if using) to get to a soft, non-sticky dough. Add 1 tablespoon of the oil and knead it in well. Taste and add more salt if you want. Cover and leave to rest for 20 minutes.

Divide the dough into 8–9 portions, then form them into balls and keep them covered.

Lightly dust the work surface with flour. Take a dough ball and flatten it slightly. Flour both sides and use a rolling pin to roll the dough out to a 20cm/8in *thepla* of medium thickness. If you want, you can stamp perfect circles out with a 20cm/8in pan lid, if you have one to hand.

Heat a dry frying pan or tawa over a medium-high heat. Transfer a *thepla* to the tawa and cook over a medium heat until a few golden spots appear on the underside, then flip it and cook until golden spots appear as before. Press the *thepla* down with a spatula for even cooking. Drizzle about ½ teaspoon oil on one side, then flip it and cook for another minute. Do the same to the other side. Remove and stack under a cloth to keep them soft until ready to serve.

MUTTON NU SHAAK

This lamb, lentil and potato curry is Gujarati comfort food. The lentils dissolve into the sauce giving it a thick, mellow texture and the tender mutton melts in the mouth – a perfect combination. *Pictured on previous page (right).*

Serves 4

- 110g/3¾oz/generous ½ cup toor dal
- 100ml/3½fl oz/scant ½ cup vegetable oil
- 200g/7oz onions, chopped
- 500g/1lb 2oz boneless mutton leg, cut into bite-size cubes
- 300g/10½oz tomatoes, chopped
- 2 tsp hot chilli powder
- 1 tsp ground turmeric
- 1 tbsp ground coriander
- 2 tsp salt
- 5 garlic cloves, crushed
- 2 tbsp chopped fresh root ginger
- 200g/7oz potatoes, diced
- 1 litre/35fl oz/4¼ cups boiling water
- 1½ tsp Garam Masala (store-bought or see page 12)
- 2 tbsp chopped fresh coriander/cilantro

Wash the lentils under cold running water, then leave to soak in plenty of fresh water for 10–15 minutes.

Heat the oil in a large pan (that has a lid) over a medium-low heat. When hot, add the onions and sauté until golden brown. Add the mutton pieces, tomatoes, chilli powder, turmeric, ground coriander, salt, garlic, ginger and diced potatoes, and stir to combine. Drain the lentils and add to the pan, then mix well and cook over a medium heat for 15 minutes, stirring occasionally.

Add the measured boiling water, cover and let everything simmer for about 1 hour until the lentils and mutton are cooked through. Taste for seasoning and add more salt or chilli, if required.

Just before serving, stir in the garam masala and fresh coriander. Serve with *Thepla* (page 203), naan or chapati and salad.

DAL DHOKLI

A traditional Gujarati one-pot dish of simmered wholemeal/wholewheat flour dumplings in a thin dal.

Serves 4

DAL
150g/5oz/scant 1 cup toor dal (split pigeon peas)
3 tbsp rapeseed/canola oil
5–6 garlic cloves, crushed
450ml/16fl oz/1¾ cups water, or as needed
1 tsp salt, or to taste
50g/1¾oz tomatoes, chopped
2–3 green chillies, slit
1 tbsp lemon juice
2 tbsp roasted peanuts, crushed
2 tbsp chopped fresh coriander/cilantro
1 tbsp ghee

DUMPLINGS
80g/3oz/½ cup wholemeal/wholewheat flour
1 tbsp gram flour/besan
¼ tsp ground turmeric
½ tsp Kashmiri chilli powder
pinch of asafoetida
⅛ tsp carom seeds/ajwain
½ tsp salt
1 tsp rapeseed/canola oil
4–5 tbsp water

TEMPERING
2 tbsp rapeseed/canola oil
½ tsp mustard seeds
½ tsp cumin seeds
1 bay leaf
2.5cm/1in cinnamon stick
1 clove
2 dried red chillies, broken in half
8–10 curry leaves
½ tsp Kashmiri chilli powder
¼ tsp ground turmeric
small pinch of asafoetida

Wash the toor dal under cold running water until the water runs clear, then leave to soak in plenty of fresh water for 15–20 minutes.

Heat the oil in a large pan over a medium heat. Add the garlic and sauté for 2–3 minutes, then add the soaked lentils, measured water and salt. Bring to the boil, then simmer until the lentils are cooked, about 15–20 minutes.

Meanwhile, make the dough for the dumplings. In a large bowl, combine the flours, turmeric, chilli powder, asafoetida, carom seeds and salt. Mix well. Add the oil and rub it in until well incorporated, then start kneading the dough, adding the water a little at a time until you have a smooth and a little stiff dough. Cover and leave to rest for 15 minutes.

Heat the oil for the tempering in a small pan over a medium-low heat. Add the mustard and cumin seeds, then once they start to crackle add the bay leaf, cinnamon stick, clove and dried chillies. Sauté for 30 seconds, then add the curry leaves, chilli powder, turmeric and asafoetida. Immediately add the tempering to the simmering dal and stir. Mix in the tomatoes, green chillies, lemon juice and crushed peanuts, and continue to simmer the dal over a low to medium heat.

Divide the dumpling dough equally in half and form into smooth balls. Use a rolling pin to roll each out to a disc, 30cm/12in in diameter. Keeping one disc covered with a clean cloth, use a sharp knife to cut the other into small diamond shapes (*dhokli*). Repeat with the second disc of dough.

Add 2–3 *dhokli* at a time into the simmering dal and stir them in so that they do not stick to each other. Don't add all the *dhokli* at once. Continue to add, then stir, until all the *dhokli* have been added. Simmer for 10–12 minutes, stirring frequently. If the dal looks dry, add more water as needed.

To finish, add the fresh coriander and ghee, and mix well. Serve hot.

SEV TAMATER KI SABZI

A *sabzi* is a type of vegetable preparation in Gujarati cuisine. Most *sabzis* are easy to prepare, simple recipes – just like this combination of *sev* (gram flour vermicelli) with tomatoes and spices, which is a particular favourite in the region. Serve with chapati or *Thepla* (see page 203).

Serves 4

- 4 tbsp rapeseed/canola oil
- ½ tsp mustard seeds
- 1 tsp cumin seeds
- 2 tsp finely chopped fresh root ginger
- 2 green chillies, finely chopped
- pinch of asafoetida
- 500g/1lb 2oz tomatoes, finely chopped, or 1 x 400g (14oz) can of chopped tomatoes
- ½ tsp ground turmeric
- ½ tsp chilli powder
- ½ tsp ground cumin
- 1 tsp ground coriander
- ½ tsp granulated sugar, or to taste
- 100ml/3½fl oz/scant ½ cup water, or as needed
- 125g/4oz *sev* (gram flour vermicelli) (use the slightly thick variety)
- 2 tbsp chopped fresh coriander/cilantro, to garnish
- salt, to taste

Heat the oil in a large pan over a low heat. Add the mustard seeds and let crackle, then add the cumin seeds and sauté for a few seconds until they change colour. Add the ginger, green chillies and asafoetida, and sauté for 10–12 seconds until the raw aroma of ginger goes away. Stir in the chopped tomatoes, then add the spice powders and mix well. Sauté for a minute, then season with salt and sugar. Continue to sauté over a low to medium heat until the tomatoes soften and become pulpy or mushy.

Stir in the measured water (if you prefer a thicker curry, add less water) and bring to a simmer. Remove from the heat and check the seasoning, adjusting the salt and sugar to taste.

Sprinkle the *sev* evenly all over the top of the curry and serve garnished with the fresh coriander.

DHOKLA

One of the most popular snacks in Gujarati cuisine, *dhokla* is a steamed savoury cake made with a fermented lentil-rice batter, topped with a spicy tempering. I like to garnish it with ghati masala, fresh coconut, pickled beetroot and pea shoots for a modernized version.

Serves 4

- 200ml/7fl oz/scant 1 cup water, plus extra if needed
- 1½ tsp ginger paste
- 1 green chilli, ground to a paste in a pestle and mortar
- ⅓ tsp salt
- 1 tsp granulated sugar
- 1 tbsp rapeseed/canola oil, plus 1 tsp for greasing
- 1 tbsp lemon juice
- 125g/4oz/generous 1 cup gram flour/besan
- ¼ tsp ground turmeric
- 1 tbsp fine semolina
- ¾ tsp Eno fruit salt (unflavoured) plus 1 tbsp water (to activate it)

TEMPERING

- 1 tbsp rapeseed/canola oil
- ¾ tsp mustard seeds
- 1 sprig of curry leaves
- 2 green chillies, slit
- ⅛ tsp asafoetida
- 1–2 tbsp granulated sugar
- ¼ tsp salt
- 150ml/5fl oz/⅔ cup water

TO SERVE

- 1 tbsp Ghati Masala (see page 13)
- 2 tbsp grated fresh coconut
- 1 tbsp finely chopped fresh coriander/cilantro leaves
- 5–6 pickled baby beetroot, each cut into 4 pieces
- 5–6 sprigs of pea shoots

Put the measured water in a bowl and add the ginger paste, green chilli paste, salt, sugar, tablespoon of oil and lemon juice. Mix well until the sugar dissolves. Set aside.

Sift the gram flour and turmeric into a large mixing bowl. Add the fine semolina and give everything a good mix. Pour in the spiced water and whisk to a thick, lump-free batter, adding more water, if needed, to make a free-flowing yet slightly thick batter. Beat the batter very well in one direction with the whisk for 2–3 minutes. To check the consistency of the batter, dip a spoon – it has to be thick enough to coat the back of the spoon but not at ribbon consistency. Set aside.

Prepare a steamer pan and/or basket. Grease the base and sides of a 13cm/5in cake pan with the teaspoon of oil. When the water in the steamer is about to come to the boil, add the Eno to the batter, then pour in the tablespoon of water to activate it. It will froth up. Quickly mix well to incorporate, running the whisk around the edges of the bowl to mix it in evenly. Immediately pour the batter into the greased pan. Place the pan in the steamer and steam for 20 minutes, or until an inserted toothpick comes out clean. Turn off the heat and leave the cake covered in the steamer for 5 minutes.

Heat the oil for tempering in a small pan. Add the mustard seeds. When they begin to crackle, add the curry leaves and green chillies. Sauté until the curry leaves turn crisp. Add the asafoetida, sugar and salt, then pour in the measured water. Bring to a rolling boil, then remove from the heat. Stir a few times to dissolve the sugar. Cover and leave to cool a little.

Remove the pan from the steamer. Leave to cool completely. When cool, use a knife to loosen the sides and invert the *dhokla* onto a plate. Cut into squares. Pour over half of the tempering, let it soak in, then pour over the rest. Sprinkle the *dhokla* with ghati masala, fresh coconut and coriander, and dot with the pieces of pickled beetroot and pea shoots.

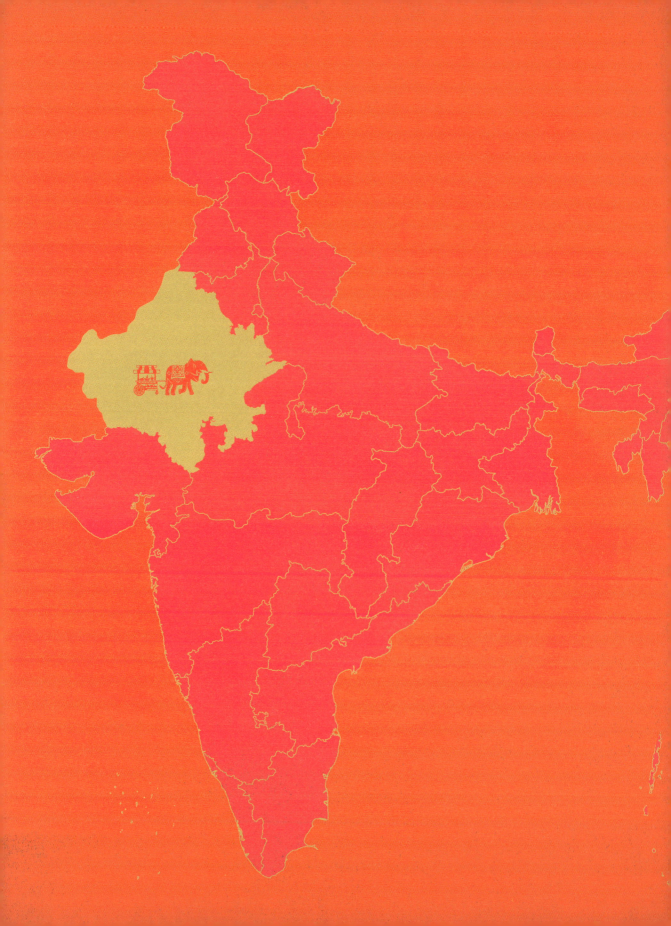

RAJASTHAN

The Rajasthan region is located in North West India. The cuisine in this area was influenced both by the warlike lifestyles of its inhabitants as well as by the availability of ingredients in such an arid land. Very little grows in the region – the extreme heat, scarcity of water and rugged terrain means that vegetation is sparse – and this led to the development of a simple, rustic, hearty cuisine unlike others in India. Wheat and millet are the staples, instead of the more ubiquitous rice found in other parts of India. Meat dishes abound, as well as the use of lentils, pulses, dried fruits and milk products (including yogurt, dried milk and ghee).

Rajasthani cuisine was heavily influenced by the Rajputs, who traditionally consumed sacrificial meat only. Their diet consisted of meat procured only via the *jhatka* method, which ensures a very quick slaughter to minimize the suffering of the animal. Lamb and mutton is popular and common dishes include *Laal Maas* (page 224) and *Junglee Maas* (page 223). Dairy-based dishes include *Gatte ki Subzi* (a curd and dumpling curry, page 220), *Jaisalmer Chana* (a yogurt-based chickpea curry, page 229) and the unique, moreish dessert made from sweetened dried milk and ghee, *Churma Laddoo* (page 230). Millet Bread (page 225) is a frequent accompaniment to meals. Vegetarians should absolutely sample the delicious *Mirchi Bada* (stuffed chillies) on page 216.

MIRCHI BADA

Rajasthani *mirchi bada* is a traditional dish of green chillies stuffed with a spicy filling that are then dipped in batter and fried to perfection. They are a popular street food snack in Jodhpur, Rajasthan, where they are also referred to as stuffed chilli cutlets. These *mirchi bada* can be served hot with mint and tamarind chutneys.

Makes 8

8 jalapeño chillies, washed and cored
neutral oil, for deep-frying
lime wedges and fresh mint leaves, to serve

STUFFING
2 potatoes, boiled and mashed
1 tsp coriander seeds, crushed
½ tsp fennel seeds, crushed
1 fresh chilli, finely chopped
½ tsp ginger paste
¾ tsp Kashmiri chilli powder
½ tsp Chaat Masala (store-bought or see page 15)
½ tsp dried mango powder/amchur
¼ tsp carom seeds/ajwain
pinch of asafoetida
2 tbsp finely chopped fresh coriander/cilantro
½ tsp salt

BATTER
150g/5oz/generous 1⅓ cups gram flour/besan
30g/1oz/3 tbsp rice flour
¼ tsp ground turmeric
½ tsp Kashmiri chilli powder
pinch of asafoetida
pinch of bicarbonate of soda/baking soda
½ tsp salt
120ml/4fl oz/½ cup water

In a large mixing bowl, combine all the stuffing ingredients and stir well, then stuff the mixture into the cored jalapeño chillies.

In a wide bowl, mix together the ingredients for the batter.

Heat a 5cm/2in depth of oil in a deep-fat fryer or heavy saucepan over a medium heat to 180°C/350°F. You'll know it's hot enough when a sprinkling of flour sizzles and floats to the surface.

When the oil is hot, dip the stuffed chillies into the batter to coat completely, then lower into the oil and deep-fry until golden and crisp, turning occasionally. Remove with a slotted spoon to drain on paper towels.

Enjoy the hot *mirchi bada* with chutneys on the side for dipping, lime wedges for squeezing and a sprinkle of fresh mint leaves.

JAIPURI KURKURI BHINDI

A spicy, tasty dish of super-crispy okra fingers, this *bhindi* recipe makes a fantastic side for everyday Indian meals and can also be served as a starter.

Serves 4

500g/1lb 2oz okra
½ tsp ground turmeric
1 tsp hot chilli powder
1 tsp ground coriander
1 tsp Garam Masala (store-bought or see page 12)
1 tsp dried mango powder/amchur
1 tsp Chaat Masala (store-bought or see page 15)
100g/3½oz/scant 1 cup gram flour/besan
2 tbsp rice flour
250ml/9fl oz/1 cup rapeseed/canola oil, for deep-frying
salt, to taste

Rinse the okra in water 3–4 times, then dry them thoroughly with paper towels. Trim off the crown and the base tips and slice each okra lengthways into 4 pieces. If you have small, thin okra, just slice in half.

Place the okra in a large bowl and sprinkle all the spice powders over, one by one. Season with salt according to taste. Gently mix to combine. Sprinkle the gram and rice flours over the okra, making sure they are evenly coated. Set aside for at least 20–30 minutes, or up to 1 hour.

Heat the oil in a deep frying pan over a medium heat. When hot, deep-fry the okra in batches until golden brown and crisp, turning them regularly so they fry evenly. Remove with a slotted spoon to drain on paper towels.

Serve immediately, perhaps with lemon wedges and a cooling raita, for dipping.

TIP These are great just as they are, but you could also garnish the okra with fresh coriander/cilantro leaves, julienned fresh root ginger or some sliced green chillies.

GATTE KI SABZI

This is a popular curry of steamed gram flour dumplings in a rich yogurt-based gravy flavoured with fenugreek. Yogurt is a key feature of many Rajasthani curries, which are known for their simplicity. Most households in the region enjoy this regularly as a wholesome vegetarian main course, with chapati or rice. It is gluten-free and delicious.

Serves 4

DUMPLINGS
- 150g/5oz/1⅓ cups gram flour/besan
- ½ tsp coriander seeds, crushed
- ¼ tsp carom seeds/ajwain
- ¼ tsp ground turmeric
- ¼ tsp Kashmiri chilli powder
- pinch of asafoetida
- pinch of salt
- 2 tbsp mustard oil
- 2 tbsp plain yogurt
- 2 tbsp water

GRAVY
- 2 tbsp mustard oil
- 1 tsp cumin seeds
- ½ tsp onion seeds
- ½ tsp carom seeds/ajwain
- ½ tsp fennel seeds
- 2 dried red chillies
- 1 bay leaf
- 250g/9oz onions, finely chopped
- 1 tsp Ginger-Garlic Paste (see page 17)
- 150g/5oz/scant ⅔ cup plain yogurt, whisked until smooth
- ¼ tsp ground turmeric
- 1 tsp Kashmiri chilli powder
- 1 tsp ground coriander
- ½ tsp ground cumin
- pinch of asafoetida
- ½ tsp salt
- 1 tsp dried fenugreek leaves
- ½ tsp Garam Masala (store-bought or see page 12)
- 2 tbsp finely chopped fresh coriander/cilantro

First, make the dumplings. In a large bowl, combine the flour with all the spices, asafoetida and salt. Add the oil and yogurt and mix thoroughly. Gradually add the measured water, kneading until you have a semi-soft dough. It should be easy to shape and there should be no cracks in the dough – if there are cracks, sprinkle on more water and continue to knead.

Divide the dough into 6 dumplings of equal size, rolling each one into a smooth ball. Using both hands, roll each ball into a cylindrical shape, about 5–6cm/2–2¼in long and 2.5cm/1in wide. Slice each cylinder into 2–3 pieces.

Bring a large pan of water to the boil and gently add the dumplings (don't overcrowd the pan – cook in batches, if necessary). When cooked, the dumplings should float to the top. Remove with a slotted spoon to a plate. Leave to cool to room temperature. Reserve 1 cup of the cooking water.

Cut the cooled dumplings into smaller, thick discs (bite-size).

Heat the mustard oil in a large pan until smoking, then reduce the heat to low and add all the whole spices and the bay leaf. Fry until they crackle, then add the onions and sauté until golden brown. Add the ginger-garlic paste and sauté until the raw smells of ginger and garlic go away. Remove from the heat and stir in the whisked yogurt. Place back over a low heat and stir continuously while you bring it to the boil. When the oil starts to separate, add the powdered spices and asafoetida, one by one. Mix well and cook for a further 1–2 minutes. Add the reserved cooking water and mix well, then add the salt and fenugreek. Simmer over a medium heat until the gravy comes to the boil, then add all of the dumplings, stirring them in very gently. Add the garam masala, mix well and simmer over a low heat for about 5–6 minutes until the gravy thickens slightly.

Remove from the heat, add the chopped coriander and serve hot.

JUNGLEE MAAS

This delicious mutton curry is slow-cooked with a unique masala paste until the meat falls off the bones. It is this very slow cooking process that is the secret behind the magic of this classic Rajasthani dish.

Serves 4

1kg/2lb 4oz mutton (or lamb or goat), cut into bite-size chunks
4 tbsp mustard oil
1½ tsp black peppercorns
1 cinnamon stick, broken into 2–3 pieces
2–3 bay leaves
1 tsp cumin seeds
3 star anise
550g/1lb 3oz onions, chopped
1 tbsp garlic paste
salt, to taste
handful of fresh coriander/cilantro leaves, to garnish

MARINADE
1½ tbsp mustard oil
1½ tbsp lime juice
1½ tsp ground turmeric
1 tbsp hot chilli powder

MAGIC MASALA
1 litre/35fl oz/4¼ cups water
7–8 dried red chillies
7–8 dried Kashmiri chillies
3 tbsp coriander seeds
5–6 green cardamom pods
1½ tsp black peppercorns
10–12 garlic cloves, peeled

Place the meat in a bowl, add the marinade ingredients and mix well. Set aside for 30 minutes.

For the magic masala, put the measured water in a large pan, add all the other masala ingredients, except for the garlic, and bring to the boil. Simmer for 10–12 minutes until the chillies are soft. Pass the mixture through a sieve/fine-mesh strainer, reserving the water in a bowl. Place all of the spices in the sieve along with the garlic cloves in a food processor and grind to a fine paste.

Heat the mustard oil in a large pan over a medium-low heat. Add the peppercorns, cinnamon, bay leaves, cumin seeds and star anise to the pan and cook for about 30 seconds, then add the onions and sauté until golden brown. Add the garlic paste and sauté for 5 minutes over a low heat. Add the marinated mutton to the pan and sauté for 10 minutes.

Add 120ml/4fl oz/½ cup of the reserved spiced water, increase the heat to medium and cook for another 15 minutes.

Add half of the ground magic masala to the pan and sauté for 10 minutes, then add the remaining ground magic masala and 800ml/28fl oz/scant 3½ cups of the reserved spiced water. Cover and cook for 1 hour–1 hour 15 minutes over a very low heat, or until the mutton is cooked through and very tender.

Season with salt to taste, garnish with fresh chopped coriander and serve with Millet Bread (see page 225).

LAAL MAAS

Red mutton is a very popular recipe from Rajasthan. It is a fiery meat curry, made with a combination of Kashmiri red chillies and other popular Rajasthani spices in an onion and yogurt sauce. It is typically very hot and rich in garlic. *Laal maas* goes very well with chapatis. I have given an extra option of infusing the curry with aromatic smoke at the end – for this you will need a small piece of charcoal and a heatproof bowl. It adds fantastic flavour, but is entirely optional.

Serves 4

100ml/3½fl oz/scant ½ cup water
8–10 dried Rajasthani mathania chillies or Kashmiri chillies, soaked in water for 20–30 minutes, then drained
150g/5oz ghee
4 black cardamom pods
6 cloves, plus 3–4 for the smoke infusion (optional)
8 green cardamom pods
2 medium cinnamon sticks
3 bay leaves
200g/7oz onions, thinly sliced
4 lamb shanks or 800g/1lb 12oz boneless lamb, diced
1 tbsp Ginger-Garlic Paste (see page 17)
1½ tsp salt, or to taste
100g/3½oz/generous ⅓ cup plain yogurt
1 tsp ground turmeric
1 tbsp Kashmiri chilli powder
1 tbsp ground coriander
1 tsp Garam Masala (store-bought or see page 12)
4–6 garlic cloves, finely chopped
piece of charcoal (optional)

TO GARNISH

2 tbsp chopped fresh coriander/cilantro
2 tbsp julienned fresh root ginger

Place the measured water in a pan, add the soaked chillies and bring to the boil. Simmer until the chillies become soft. Let cool, then strain (reserving the water). Grind the chillies to a fine paste in a food processor.

Heat most of the ghee (keep back 2 tablespoons for later) in a large, deep pan (that has a lid) over a high heat. Add the whole spices and bay leaves, and sauté briefly, then add the onions and fry until browned. Add the lamb and sauté until golden on the outside. Add the ginger-garlic paste and cook for another couple of minutes, then add the salt, chilli paste and half of the reserved chilli cooking water. Cook, stirring, for another 6–8 minutes.

In a mixing bowl, combine the remaining chilli water with the yogurt, turmeric, chilli powder, ground coriander, garam masala and a pinch of salt. Add to the lamb curry, cover and cook over a very low heat for 1½ hours.

Heat 1 tablespoon of the remaining ghee in a small pan, add the chopped garlic and fry until browned. Add to the curry and mix well.

As an extra optional touch, place a piece of live charcoal in a small heatproof bowl and place the bowl in the curry. Pour over the last tablespoon of ghee and 3–4 cloves. Immediately cover the pan with the lid and allow the smoke to infuse the *laal maas* for about 3–4 minutes. Remove the charcoal bowl from the curry and check the seasoning.

Serve hot, garnished with fresh coriander and julienned ginger.

MILLET BREAD

This wholegrain millet bread is naturally gluten-free and vegan. It is soft, fluffy, moist – and so easy to make! *Pictured overleaf (left).*

Makes 6 breads

200g/7oz/1⅓ cups millet flour
60g/2oz/½ cup gram flour/besan
1 tsp carom seeds/ajwain
1 tsp salt
3 tbsp rapeseed/canola oil
up to 200ml/7fl oz/scant 1 cup water

In a large bowl, mix together all of the ingredients to make a dough, adding the water slowly and gradually, using only enough to bring the ingredients together into a dough. Knead the dough with your palm slowly for 5–6 minutes until soft and pliable.

Divide the dough into 6 balls of equal size and flatten with your hands, then roll out with a rolling pin to even, thin circles, 10–12cm/4–5in in diameter.

Cook the breads on a dry, hot pan until speckled with black on both sides.

KESAR MURGH

Saffron chicken is a Rajasthani delicacy. Moderately spiced and rich, it is a popular dish, traditionally served with tandoori roti or millet breads. *Pictured on previous page (right).*

Serves 4

- 100ml/3½fl oz/scant ½ cup rapeseed/canola oil
- 4–5 cloves
- 5 green cardamom pods
- 2 bay leaves
- 1 tbsp Ginger-Garlic Paste (see page 17)
- 200g/7oz Fried Onion Paste (see page 17)
- 1 tsp ground coriander
- 2 tbsp cashew nut paste (or cashews soaked in hot water, then blended to a smooth paste)
- 800g/1lb 12oz skinless, boneless chicken thighs
- 100g/3½oz/generous ⅓ cup plain yogurt
- 2 green chillies, slit
- 1 tsp white pepper
- ½ tbsp hot chilli powder
- 1 tbsp salt, or to taste
- ½ tsp saffron strands dissolved in 4 tbsp milk
- ½ tbsp Garam Masala (store-bought or see page 12)
- 3 tbsp double/heavy cream
- 2 tbsp chopped fresh coriander/cilantro, to garnish

Heat the oil in a large pan over a medium-low heat. Add the whole spices and bay leaves to the pan, and sauté briefly, then add the ginger-garlic and onion pastes. Fry over a low heat until the oil separates. Add the ground coriander and cashew nut paste, and mix well.

Stir in the chicken thighs, then add the yogurt, green chillies, white pepper, chilli powder, salt and saffron milk. Bring to the boil, then reduce to a simmer for 15–20 minutes until the chicken is cooked through.

Add the garam masala and keep stirring, cooking for a final 5–6 minutes. Stir in the cream, then remove from the heat.

Serve hot, garnished with the fresh coriander.

JAISALMER CHANA

This creamy black chickpea/*kala chana* curry is a traditional dish originating from a city called Jaisalmer in Rajasthan. Yogurt and gram flour-based curries are a speciality of the region.

Serves 4

- 375g/13oz/1½ cups plain yogurt
- 4 tbsp gram flour/besan
- 2 tbsp hot chilli powder
- 2 tbsp Garam Masala (store-bought or see page 12)
- ½ tsp ground turmeric
- 1 tbsp ground coriander
- ¼ tsp plus a large pinch of asafoetida
- 500ml/17fl oz/2 cups water, or more as needed
- 2 tbsp ghee
- 2 green chillies, finely chopped
- 2 x 400g/14oz cans of black chickpeas/*kala chana*/Bengal gram, drained and rinsed, then drained again
- 1 tsp cumin seeds
- salt, to taste

In a large bowl, combine the yogurt, gram flour, 1 teaspoon of the chilli powder, 1 teaspoon of the garam masala, the turmeric, coriander and the ¼ teaspoon of asafoetida. Whisk well, then add the measured water and whisk again. Set aside.

Heat the ghee in a large pan over a medium heat. Add the large pinch of asafoetida and chopped green chillies and sauté briefly. Add half of the chickpeas. Crush the remaining half with the end of a rolling pin, then add those too to the pan. Mix well. Add the remaining chilli powder and garam masala, and season with salt, to taste. Add the cumin seeds and sauté for a further 2–3 minutes. Add the yogurt mixture to the pan and cook until the gravy thickens. If the gravy looks too thick, you could add up to 250ml/9fl oz/1 cup more water, then bring to the boil and simmer until the sauce is the consistency you prefer.

Transfer to a serving bowl and serve hot.

CHURMA LADDOO

Churma ladoo is a typical Rajasthani sweet made with wholemeal/wholewheat flour, dried milk, ghee and nuts. It has a crumbly, flaky texture and a gentle sweetness. Both the dough and *mawa/khoya* are cooked first before they are crumbled and mixed together, and are then rolled in crushed nuts. It's easy to make and very delicious – guaranteed to make everyone happy. The dried milk product known as *mawa*, or *khoya*, can be made from scratch, but it is so time-consuming, that I would always recommend you buy it at an Indian grocery store or online.

Makes 8

350g/12oz/2⅓ cups wholemeal/wholewheat flour
400g/14oz ghee
100ml/3½fl oz/scant ½ cup milk
200g/7oz *mawa/khoya* (dried milk product – buy ready-made at Indian grocery stores or online)
350g/12oz/scant 3 cups icing/confectioners' sugar
100g/3½oz almonds and cashews or pistachios, finely chopped (optional)
finely chopped almonds and pistachios, to decorate

Place the flour in a wide bowl and rub 125g/4½oz of the ghee into the flour so that it is completely coated. Add the milk and knead the mixture into a tight dough. Divide the dough into 12 equal-sized balls (around the size of a tennis ball) and press them with your palm to flatten them a little bit.

Heat the remaining ghee in a frying pan over a low-medium heat. Add the dumplings to the pan in batches and fry for about 10–15 minutes until golden brown all over. Remove with a slotted spoon to drain on paper towels. Reserve the ghee in the pan.

Once the dumplings are cool enough to touch, crumble them up by hand to make a fine powder (or whizz in a food processor). Set aside.

Heat a dry frying pan over a medium heat, add the *mawa/khoya* and dry-roast, stirring constantly, until it is light brown in colour and smells fragrant. Remove from the heat and place in a bowl to cool down.

When cool enough to handle, crumble the roasted *mawa/khoya* into small pieces by hand and leave to cool for a further 10 minutes, then transfer it to a food processor and grind to a fine powder. Add the icing sugar and mix well, then add 175ml/6fl oz/¾ cup of the reserved ghee and mix well.

Transfer the mixture to a large bowl and add the dumpling powder along with the finely chopped nuts (if using). Mix well. Take a handful of the mixture and press to shape it into firm, round balls. Roll them in the finely chopped almonds and pistachios to decorate before serving.

The *ladoos* will keep in an airtight container for a few days.

ABOUT THE AUTHOR

Rohit Ghai's love affair with food began in his mother's kitchen, in his native Punjab, India. He went on to study Hotel Management at the Institute of Culinary Management in Gwalior, which is affiliated with Pusa University in New Delhi. He then trained at two of the biggest hotel groups in India – the Taj Hotel and Resort Group and the Oberoi Hotel Group. After moving to the UK, Rohit worked in and headed kitchens at some of London's leading Indian restaurants, including Benares, Trishna, Gymkhana, Hoppers, Jamavar and Bombay Bustle. Rohit is the first Indian chef to have won a Michelin star. In 2018, he launched his first solo London restaurant, Kutir, followed by KoolCha, and then Manthan in Mayfair. Most recently, he opened Rivayat restaurant at the Oberoi hotel in Marrakesh.

@chefrohitghai | www.rohitghai.co.uk

ACKNOWLEDGEMENTS

I would like to express my great appreciation to some of my food heros: Jaswinder Singh Teja (Oberoi Hotels) and the late Pankaj Mehra (Indian Master Chef, Oberoi Hotels). Their work has inspired me over many years and they have been instrumental in building my perception of curries across the globe. I would like to also offer my special thanks to my team of chefs at Kutir and Manthan, who have been very supportive during the journey of my second book, *Yatra*.

Special thanks go to my publisher Fiona Robertson, commissioning editor Ella Chappell, project editor Emily Preece-Morrison, photographer Gareth Morgans, food stylist Jennifer Joyce, prop stylist Julie Patmore, head of design Karen Smith and all the team members of Watkins Publishing, who have been hugely supportive in the delivery of this book.

And considerable thanks go to my lovely wife Akansha and amazing (naughty) daughters Trisha and Tanisha, who have been an immense encouragement and support, even when the little ones had to sacrifice their play time over the weekends to make this book happen on time.

INDEX

A
aamras with saffron *pooris* 190
almonds: *churma laddoo* 230
    double ka meetha 128
    navaratan korma 56
    rose *sandesh* 107
    shahi tukda 66
aloo posto 99
ambotik 167
Amritsari fish 26
amti dal 185
Andhra chicken fry 116
Andhra lamb masala 123
Andhra Pradesh 8, 110–29
Andhra spice mix 116
aubergines/eggplants: *baghare baingan* 117
    begun bhaja 92
    bharli vangi 181
    khichdi 199
    litti chokha 75
    macher jhol 98

B
baghare baingan 117
balchão, prawns 159
banana leaves: *karimeen pollichathu* 134
bebinca 168
beef, *nadan* 138
begun bhaja 92
Bengali garam masala 13
berries: berry chutney 108
    semiyan payasam 148
bhaja, *begun* 92
bhapa doi 108
bharli vangi 181
bhindi, Jaipuri *kurkuri* 218
Bihar 8, 68–87
Bihari *aloo bhujiya* 82
Bihari *besan ka sabji* 78
Bihari *chana dal puri* 83
Bihari chicken curry 79
biryanis: biryani masala 16
    chicken biryani 62
    Hyderabadi vegetable *dum biryani* 120–1
black chickpeas/*kala chana*/Bengal gram: Jaisalmer *chana* 229
Bombay mix: *jhalmuri* 72
breads: Bihari *chana dal puri* 83
    chapati 21
    double ka meetha 128
    luchhi 106
    millet bread 225
    mooli paratha 35
    naan 21
    saffron *pooris* 190
    shahi tukda 66
    sheermal 57
    thepla 203
bulgur wheat: *haleem* 127
burani raita 20
butter chicken 33

C
cabbage *thoran* 137
cafreal spice mix 157
cake: *bebinca* 168
carrots: Hyderabadi vegetable *dum biryani* 120–1
    Keralan vegetable stew 140
    thayir sadam 145
cashews: *churma laddoo* 230
    double ka meetha 128
    dum ka murgh 64
    navaratan korma 56
    poha 175
    semiyan payasam 148
cauliflower: cauliflower pickle 20

Keralan vegetable stew 140
  navaratan korma 56
chaat masala 15
Champaran mutton curry 76
chana dal (yellow split peas):
  Bihari *chana dal puri* 83
  haleem 127
  shami kebab 48
chapati 21
chicken: Andhra chicken fry 116
  Bihari chicken curry 79
  butter chicken 33
  chicken biryani 62
  chicken *rezala* 96
  chicken tikka 33
  chicken tikka *mirza husnoo* 51
  dal chicken 184
  dum ka murgh 64
  kesar murgh 228
  Malvani chicken curry 189
  murghanu shaak 202
  murgi jhol 95
  nadan kozhi 141
  tandoori chicken 28
  xacuti chicken 154
chickpeas: Jaisalmer *chana* 229
chillies: *aloo posto* 99
  ambotik 167
  fish *cafreal* 157
  laal maas 224
  mirchi bada 216
  prawns *balchão* 159
  sorak 163
  xacuti chicken 154
chingri malai kari 102
chokha, litti 75
churma laddoo 230
chutney: berry chutney 108
  coconut chutney 18
  green chutney 176–8
  mint and coriander chutney 18

sweet tamarind chutney 176–8
  tomato chutney 19
cloves: *laung lata* 86
coconut: *baghare baingan* 117
  coconut chutney 18
  khandvi 196
  nadan beef 138
  xacuti chicken 154
coconut milk: *bebinca* 168
  chingri malai kari 102
  egg *kurma* 124
  Goan fish curry 162
  Keralan fish curry 144
  Keralan vegetable stew 140
  nadan kozhi 141
  semiyan payasam 148
condensed milk: *bhapa doi* 108
  double *ka meetha* 128
coriander seeds: *xacuti* chicken 154
coriander/cilantro leaves: fish *cafreal* 157
  green chutney 176–8
  mint and coriander chutney 18
cranberries: *bhapa doi* 108
cucumber: *thayir sadam* 145
curry: *ambotik* 167
  baghare baingan 117
  Bihari *besan ka sabji* 78
  Bihari chicken curry 79
  butter chicken 33
  Champaran mutton curry 76
  chicken *rezala* 96
  chingri malai kari 102
  dal chicken 184
  dum ka murgh 64
  egg *kurma* 124
  fish *salan* 65
  gatte ki sabzi 219
  Goan fish curry 162
  Jaisalmer *chana* 229
  junglee maas 223
  Keralan fish curry 144

kesar murgh 228
laal maas 224
macher jhol 98
Malvani chicken curry 189
mangsher jhol 94
murghanu shaak 202
murgi jhol 95
mutton *nu shaak* 206
nadan kozhi 141
palak paneer 39
poori subzi 53
pork vindaloo 160
sev tamater ki sabzi 209
sorak 163
varutharacha mutton curry 142

D

dal: *amti dal* 185
   dal chicken 184
   dal dhokla 207
   dal makhani 34
   khatti dal 126
dal puri, Bihari chana 83
dhokla 210
double *ka meetha* 128
dough balls: *litti chokha* 75
drinks: mango lassi 40
   neer mor 149
dum ka murgh 64
dumplings: Bihari *besan ka sabji* 78
   dal dhokla 207
   gatte ki sabzi 219
   vada pav 176–8

E

eggs: egg *kurma* 124
   nargisi kofta 54

F

fenugreek: *thepla* 203
fish: Amritsari fish 26
   banana leaf fish 134
   fish *cafreal* 157
   fish *salan* 65
   Goan fish curry 162
   Keralan fish curry 144
   macher jhol 98
   recheado fish fry 158
flatbreads *see* breads
fritters: *begun bhaja* 92

G

garam masala 12
   Bengali *garam masala* 13
garlic: Champaran mutton curry 76
   fish *cafreal* 157
   ginger-garlic paste 17
   pork vindaloo 160
   prawns *balchão* 159
gatte ki sabzi 219
ghati masala 13
   ghati masala prawns 180
ginger: Champaran mutton curry 76
   ginger-garlic paste 17
   prawns *balchão* 159
Goa 9, 150–69
Goan fish curry 162
goat: *shami* kebab 48
gram flour/besan: Bihari *besan ka sabji* 78
green chutney 176–8
Gujarat 10, 192–211

H

haleem 127
Hyderabadi vegetable *dum biryani* 120–1

J

Jaipuri *kurkuri bhindi* 218
Jaisalmer *chana* 229
jalapeño chillies: *mirchi bada* 216
jhalmuri 72
jhol: *macher jhol* 98
  mangsher jhol 94
  murgi jhol 95
junglee maas 223

K

kadhi 200
kala masala 14
  mutton *kala masala* 179
karimeen pollichathu 134
kebab, *shami* 48
Kerala 9, 130–49
Keralan fish curry 144
Keralan vegetable stew 140
kesar murgh 228
khandvi 196
khatti dal 126
kheer, *makhana* 84
khichdi 199
kidney beans: *rajma rasila* 30
kofta, *nargisi* 54
kokum (black mangosteen): Keralan fish curry 144
Kolhapuri *masala* 16
korma, *navaratan* 56
kurma, egg 124

L

laal maas 224
lamb: Andhra lamb masala 123
  laal maas 224
  nihari 61
  saag gosht 29
  tunday kabab 50
lassi, mango 40
laung lata 86
lentils: *amti dal* 185

dal chicken 184
dal makhani 34
khatti dal 126
masoor dal 104
moong dal halwa 43
mutton *nu shaak* 206
litti chokha 75
lotus seeds/fox nuts: *makhana kheer* 84
luchhi 106

M

maas: *junglee maas* 223
  laal maas 224
macher jhol 98
magic masala 223
Maharashtra 10, 170–91
makhana kheer 84
makhani: *dal makhani* 34
  makhani sauce 33
Malvani chicken curry 189
Malvani masala 189
mango: *aamras* with saffron *pooris* 190
  mango lassi 40
mangsher jhol 94
masalas: Andhra lamb masala 123
  Bengali garam masala 13
  biryani masala 16
  chaat masala 15
  garam masala 12
  ghati masala 13
  ghati masala prawns 180
  kala masala 14
  Kolhapuri *masala* 16
  magic masala 223
  Malvani masala 189
  masala paste 159
  mutton *kala* masala 179
  nihari masala 61
  panch phoran 14
  poha magic masala 15
  recheado masala 158

masoor dal 104
mawa/khoya (dried milk product):
   churma laddoo 230
   laung lata 86
milk: double ka meetha 128
   makhana kheer 84
   shahi tukda 66
millet bread 225
mint and coriander chutney 18
mirchi bada 216
mooli paratha 35
moong dal/mung beans: haleem 127
   moong dal halwa 43
   pesarattu 114
murgh, kesar 228
murghanu shaak 202
murgi jhol 95
mushrooms:
   Hyderabadi vegetable dum biryani 120–1
mutton: Champaran mutton curry 76
   haleem 127
   junglee maas 223
   mangsher jhol 94
   mutton kala masala 179
   mutton nu shaak 206
   nargisi kofta 54
   varutharacha mutton curry 142

N

naan 21
nadan beef 138
nadan kozhi 141
nargisi kofta 54
navaratan korma 56
neer mor 149
nihari 61
noodles: semiyan payasam 148
nuts: laung lata 86
   rose sandesh 107

O

okra: Jaipuri kurkuri bhindi 218
onions: ambotik 167
   Bihari chicken curry 79
   Champaran mutton curry 76
   egg kurma 124
   fried onion paste 17
   Hyderabadi vegetable dum biryani 120–1
   junglee maas 223
   Keralan fish curry 144
   macher jhol 98
   mutton kala masala 179
   nadan beef 138
   paneer kolhapuri 186
   pork vindaloo 160

P

palak paneer 39
pancakes: pesarattu 114
panch phoran 14
paneer: navaratan korma 56
   palak paneer 39
   paneer kolhapuri 186
paratha, mooli 35
pastes: fried onion paste 17
   ginger-garlic paste 17
patties: shami kebab 48
   tunday kabab 50
peanuts: baghare baingan 117
   bharli vangi 181
   poha 175
peas: Hyderabadi vegetable dum biryani 120–1
   Keralan vegetable stew 140
   khichdi 199
pesarattu 114
pickle, cauliflower 20
pistachios: shahi tukda 66
poha 175
poha magic masala 15
poori: poori subzi 53
   saffron pooris 190

poppy seeds: *aloo posto* 99
   chicken *rezala* 96
   dum ka murgh 64
   egg *kurma* 124
pork vindaloo 160
potatoes: *aloo posto* 99
   Bihari *aloo bhujiya* 82
   Hyderabadi vegetable *dum biryani* 120–1
   Keralan vegetable stew 140
   khichdi 199
   litti chokha 75
   mangsher jhol 94
   mirchi bada 216
   murghanu shaak 202
   murgi jhol 95
   mutton *nu shaak* 206
   navaratan korma 56
   pesarattu 114
   poha 175
   poori subzi 53
   vada pav 176–8
prawns/shrimp: *ambotik* 167
   chingri malai kari 102
   ghati masala prawns 180
   prawns *balchão* 159
puffed lotus seeds (*phool makhana*/fox nuts):
   makhana kheer 84
puffed rice: *jhalmuri* 72
Punjab 8, 22–43

R
raisins: *semiyan payasam* 148
raita, *burani* 20
Rajasthan 10, 212–31
rajma rasila 30
recheado fish fry 158
rezala, chicken 96
rice: chicken biryani 62
   Hyderabadi vegetable *dum biryani* 120–1
   khichdi 199
   thayir sadam 145
rose petals: *bhapa doi* 108
   rose *sandesh* 107

S
saag gosht 29
sabzi: *gatte ki sabzi* 219
   sev tamater ki sabzi 209
saffron *pooris* 190
salan, fish 65
semiyan payasam 148
sev tamater ki sabzi 209
shaak: *murghanu shaak* 202
   mutton *nu shaak* 206
shahi tukda 66
shami kebab 48
sheermal 57
skewers: chicken tikka *mirza husnoo* 51
   fish *cafreal* 157
   xacuti chicken 154
sorak 163
spice mixes: Andhra spice mix 116
   cafreal spice mix 157
   panch phoran 14
   see also masalas
spinach: *palak paneer* 39
   saag gosht 29
stews: *haleem* 127
   Keralan vegetable stew 140
   nihari 61
subzi, *poori* 53
sweet tamarind chutney 176–8

T

tadka 126
tamarind: *baghare baingan* 117
   sweet tamarind chutney 176–8
tandoori chicken 28
thayir sadam 145
thepla 203
thoran, cabbage 137
tikka, chicken 33
tomatoes: Andhra chicken fry 116
   egg *kurma* 124
   Keralan fish curry 144
   khatti dal 126
   macher jhol 98
   makhani sauce 33
   mutton *nu shaak* 206
   paneer kolhapuri 186
   pork vindaloo 160
   prawns *balchão* 159
   sev tamater ki sabzi 209
   tomato chutney 19
toor dal (split pigeon peas): *amti dal* 185
   dal dhokla 207
   haleem 127
   khatti dal 126
   khichdi 199
   mutton *nu shaak* 206
tunday kabab 50

U

urad dal (whole black lentils): *dal makhani* 34
   haleem 127
Uttar Pradesh 8, 44–67

V

vada pav 176–8
varutharacha mutton curry 142
vegetables:
   Hyderabadi vegetable *dum biryani* 120–1
   Keralan vegetable stew 140
vermicelli noodles: *semiyan payasam* 148
vindadoo, pork 160

W

West Bengal 8, 88–109

X

xacuti chicken 154

Y

yogurt: *bhapa doi* 108
   Bihari chicken curry 79
   burani raita 20
   chicken biryani 62
   chicken *tikka mirza husnoo* 51
   gatte ki sabzi 219
   Hyderabadi vegetable *dum biryani* 120–1
   Jaisalmer *chana* 229
   kadhi 200
   mango lassi 40
   neer mor 149
   tandoori chicken 28
   thayir sadam 145
   xacuti chicken 154